HOW TO HUSTLE

Going All In Without Losing Yourself

JESSIE PACHAN

DEDICATED TO

Alexis, Hannah, and Finley – I am so proud of each of you and love watching you grow. I hope you chase after everything you want in life no matter how scary it feels. Go live your best lives, without fear or apology. Your dad and I will always be here.

TABLE OF CONTENTS

Introduction 1

PART ONE: *What is Hustle*................................ 5

    1: Leave Hustlers Alone................................ 7

    2: Own Your Decisions.............................. 21

    3: Hustle Vs Reflection 33

PART TWO: *The Four Areas of Life*................ 45

    4: Area One: Spritial and Emotional 47

    5. Area Two: Physical................................ 61

    6: Area Three: Personal Connections......... 73

    7: Area Four: Financial 91

    8: The Disciplines 105

PART THREE: *Betting on Yourself* 121

    9: Love Yourself Despite, Not Because 123

    10: Betting on Yourself 131

    11: Get Ready for What You Don't Have... Yet 151

    12: Two Sides of Fear.............................. 159

    13: Peace and Balance 175

INTRODUCTION

As I write this, David Goggins is dominating book shelves, podcasts and social media. As an ex-Navy Seal, New York Times Best-Selling Author, and an overall badass, he recently released his second book, *Never Finished,* and everyone is inspired to run for 24 hours straight. With two broken legs. Carrying a boat. While fighting a bear.

While many may be inspired, very few will actually attempt the things he's done. Very few will lose 106 pounds in three months. Very few will finish a 100-mile run with broken bones in both feet. Very few will push themselves to a level that makes others envy their superhuman DNA, as most are only inspired to dream about what they are capable of.

And just like others, he inspires me. I am fascinated by his drive and perseverance, and could listen to his outrageous stories and interviews all day. His words motivate me to get my shoes on and push through a workout I didn't feel like doing. His voice screams in my head when I'm ready to quit, and helps me squeeze out another half-mile. But no matter how much Goggins I listen to, I just can't seem to lose this same five pounds.

About a year ago, I went to dinner with a friend and skipped the appetizer because, "I wanted to lose five pounds." Recently, we went to dinner again, and again, I skipped the appetizer for the same reason.

She remembered the first dinner and asked how much more weight I was trying to lose. "No more, this is the same five pounds," I admitted.

I'm not looking to inspire people to go all in like David Goggins. Since there's really no such thing as superhuman DNA, that means David is just a man who has committed to doing the things most people can't. I'm looking to inspire people to do the things most people *won't*. Things that are small and easy. Things that anyone can do. Everyone *should* do. I will probably never run a single mile on two broken legs, even if a bear was chasing me. I'm more likely to just lie down and let the bear seal my fate.

Between three kids, soccer and softball practices, the job, the spouse, the laundry, and the peanut butter crusted door knobs, it's difficult to ensure you're building a stable future when you're just trying to survive the days. There's a constant struggle between "good enough" and "I should be doing more," and guilt likes to insert itself into all of those internal dialogues.

As a parent, I have fought battles in my head when deciding between much-needed grocery shopping or work. Work brings me joy. Navigating a cart past indecisive strangers brings me anxiety. Admitting that sometimes I choose work, and we eat mac and cheese from a cup brings judgment from others. How do we win?

This book is my journey from 'trainwreck' to success. How I took back control of my days, not by doing less, but by adding more. I began including small things that matter so I'm better equipped to handle the big things that interrupt my day.

I learned how to hustle. Not just in my career, but in my life, relationships, and finances, as well as my values and beliefs. If you are inspired by someone like David Goggins, but function more like a Jessie Pachan, then this book is for you.

PART ONE

WHAT IS HUSTLE

1

LEAVE HUSTLERS ALONE

It's 5 p.m. The work day is over for most people. I get off the phone with my boss and I sit in silence. I'm not sure if it's a few seconds or a few minutes, but it's enough time to look up and see the email notifications pile up again.

At this point, I'm not sure of my next move. I don't know why I am blaming him for all of this. Maybe it's because he promised this wasn't going to happen. I knew it wasn't a promise he could keep and it definitely wasn't anything that could be predicted. The weight of what's coming hits me and I finally break. The tears start.

Before this moment, I hadn't cried in a long time. Crying used to be my go-to emotion, but I learned that doesn't get you far up the ladder in the financial industry (that's another book, we're not going there). If you want to be taken seriously and seen as a leader, you need to master your emotions, especially as a female. I know that's true because once I grasped this concept, I received greater results in my relationships and additional leadership opportunities in my career. But for right now, I have too many emotions to gain control of any of them. I'm defeated. I'm overwhelmed. And I know that for the next period of time, I won't have a spare minute to think about my feelings again. Although no one could predict this was going to last eighteen months, somehow, I knew it was going to be a long road.

I got up from my desk, put on my work out clothes, pick my music, and hit the treadmill.

That day, I ran one of my fastest two miles ever. I began my run with tears streaming down my face, but ended with new strength and determination to take full advantage of what was about to take place.

THE BIGGEST BOOM

Interest rates had been sliding with threats of COVID-19 spreading across the globe. They were lingering in the 3% range and, as a mortgage loan officer, I could tolerate that. It was a great opportunity to make some good money. I knew it was going to be a lot of work, but at these rates, my team and I could manage the pipeline, keep things moving, and still provide excellent customer service. We knew if we saw anything in the 2% range, demand would explode well beyond our manpower, our current clients would try to find lower rates elsewhere, and although we could easily rebuild, did we even have the capacity and energy to meet such an economic whirlwind?

In a meeting, our president had told us not to panic. He reminded us that low rates are a gift and encouraged us to take advantage before it was too late. Do the best we could to manage our workload and handle whatever comes up. I believe his exact words were, "You've all seen rates drop before. I promise we're not going to see anything under 3%, so chill out."

He was wrong.

For the next 18 months, the historically low rates didn't let up, eventually landing where my boss assured us they wouldn't. They dropped multiple times and clients we closed at 3.5% were refinancing again and again as each opportunity presented itself. During that period, I don't remember taking an evening or weekend off. I can tell you that I did drive my kids to every practice and was always where I needed to be as a parent, but I was back on the phone between each family event.

This was my fourth refinance boom, and it was by far my biggest. I soon realized my boss was right – we may never see anything like this again. With people walking away with once-in-a-lifetime mortgage terms, how long could it be before we see another influx like this? There will always be people buying or refinancing homes, but the money would never be this easy in my career again.

Since my income is 100% commission, I took my boss' advice – I went all in and took full advantage. The texts between my husband and I looked like this:

> **Me:** Rates dropped AGAIN!!!!!!
>
> **Scott:** What do you need?
>
> **Me:** I'll be in my office. Can you get the kids off the bus and slip a sandwich under the door from time to time?

I was fortunate to have the help, but with or without it, I was committed to finding a way to get in as many hours as I could.

Why was Scott okay with me working like this?

Because he knows daily balance is bullshit. There are going to be days when the family time will be short, and other days when we all need a break from each other. He knows that our marriage and family are not strong because we spend a certain amount of time together, but because we each step up and fill in each other's gaps when needed. And I needed him right then. Luckily, being self-employed, he had the flexibility to lighten his schedule in order to accommodate mine.

Why was I okay with working like this?

Because I know the more uncomfortable that I am earlier in life, the more comfortable we will all be later. This impacts my whole family for the better. Maybe we could pay off the mortgage early and travel together. Maybe this would allow for more college options for our daughters. Our goals weren't going to happen overnight. It was going to take many seasons of life, and we were in one of them now.

I was also sure I could handle it mentally without putting a strain on my family this time around. Since I had experienced this influx in business three times before, I knew how to prepare my body and mind for the stress that awaited me. I woke up early each morning to lay the groundwork for my day. This started with a little time journaling, then a quick jog in order to build energy and endurance, and clear out my head. Most importantly, even though I worked a lot, the work was flexible and I was still able to check in on our girls to hear about their day. Despite the workload, I felt I had complete control of my life and was balanced in all important areas – although they weren't each given the same amount of attention on any given day. This balance took years of trial and error to accomplish, but I'll summarize the process for you in one book.

WHAT EXCITES YOU?

By this fourth refi boom, I also knew one thing about myself that many haven't figured out in their own lives. I knew what excited me in my work. I loved the fast-paced, high-stress work days where I could exercise all my strengths and weaknesses on a large scale. This included being on the hunt for new clients, managing current clients, problem-solving, and putting out, as well as preventing fires both on the front lines and behind the scenes. I was never sure how I was going to 'handle it all,' yet I decided to view figuring it out as a thrill instead of a burden.

This wasn't always the case. Over the years, I listened to so many complain about the stress and responsibility of their job only to miss it when it was gone. I had been in that group initially, upset and frustrated with the issues that came up, only to beg for the problems to return once work slowed down. I was going to enjoy every minute this time around. This shift in mindset from complaining to appreciating created a new passion, not only in my career, but in my life.

Most people never stop to think about what is exciting about their work. They immediately view work as a chore and lack the ability to find anything good in the job they do. They dislike even the tasks they excel at, without any thought to understanding and developing their strengths. They hear others complain and they join in the negativity, never giving their job a chance to be fulfilling.

On the contrary, many love what they do and can do it all day, but hear phrases like "overachiever," "workaholic," or "your priorities are messed up," and they shy away from going all in. There's a level of guilt associated with these phrases, which may lead someone to squash their passion. While reflection is good, it should be done by us, not by outside voices.

It took years, but I could eventually identify what parts of my job I loved, what parts were taking a toll, and what adjustments I needed to make to stay excited about the work. Instead of trying to avoid the stress that constantly reared its ugly head, I started to embrace it, and eventually began to dominate it. By taking the time to diagnose the cause of any stress and anxiety, I was shocked to realize – most of it was self-induced.

I used to panic when a client was upset with the process and wanted to talk. I dodged their phone calls until I was forced to face their frustrations. But when I finally did, we'd reach a resolution, and over time, I found that I excelled at these difficult exchanges. I eventually began to enjoy the challenge. My fear of confrontation became my strength as a professional. Now I no longer avoid tough conversations – I pick up the phone first alleviating the anxiety that comes with procrastination.

By embracing my unique abilities in dreaded situations, I learned to see these stressors as fun and exciting – my chance to shine.

THE FIRST BOOM

My goal is to save you the years I spent resisting instead of embracing. Obstacles and stress are happening no matter how hard you try to avoid both. Will you approach each with dread or seize each with determination? Your work may not have the highs and lows that I have experienced in the financial industry, but there will be seasons in your life when you will have exciting opportunities that require energy and endurance to go all in. Will you be ready?

Fourteen years earlier, during my first refinance boom, I was spiraling into a dark place. The work never slowed down, and I was constantly tired and overwhelmed. I didn't have any boundaries with clients. I wasn't spending time for myself each morning, so the day started with emails, feeling behind, and never having a grip of my days. I was heading for burnout and hit it fast. Quickly becoming angry and resentful, I became short with clients and grew annoyed answering the same questions all the time.

My inability to control what was happening at work was impacting my family life also.

During this time, I ran into a family friend, James, at the grocery store and we briefly caught up about how things were going. He caught me off guard when he said, "You really need time off. You shouldn't work this hard."

A bit older than me and recently divorced, James had reached a point in his life where he was reflecting and slowing down. In his prime, he was labeled a workaholic, among other aholics that had caused his divorce. He really believed he was being helpful and was trying to prevent me from making his past mistakes, but it wasn't his hustling that caused them – it was who he became while he hustled. It was the stress, anger, not being present for his wife, as well as some of his other habits that caused the end of his marriage. His ex had supported his career ventures. She liked the security and understood what was required to get his business off the ground, but she had had enough of who he'd become during this time. I just needed to make sure I wasn't becoming the same.

So, while his advice was well-intentioned, he was just in a different phase of life winding down his hustle while I was just ramping things up. Until I understood this, I struggled with James' recommendation to take a break. Did I really need to? Was my marriage imploding and I was too busy to see it? I felt involved in my children's lives, but did they see me as absent? Spoiler alert – they didn't.

I didn't want to hear about slowing down, but looking back, I didn't need to. He wasn't right. I knew I'd get a break when the rates went back up. The work wasn't the issue; my ability to handle it was. I needed to tweak a few areas in my life so I could keep going.

ADDING MORE EQUALS LESS

I ultimately realized that my burnout came from a place of being overwhelmed and feeling a complete lack of control in my life. I was constantly worried I was forgetting something. My house was a mess and I couldn't remember the last time I'd changed my socks. I knew something had to give. Ironically, I didn't want a change because I was overwhelmed. I wanted a change so I could take my business to the next level while keeping my personal life intact.

I picked up books on success, listened to podcasts, and got a life coach. Even though I would fall asleep reading, couldn't get through two minutes of a podcast without interruptions, and stressed about going to my coaching sessions during valuable work time, I picked up a few tips. Ultimately, this compilation of knowledge led me to a huge discovery.

I would need to add *more* to my life in order to reduce the things I didn't want. More work in the right areas would eliminate the wrongs that were consuming me.

Whether you call it the seven pillars of life, the eight dimensions of well-being, the nine this, or the twelve that, what I'm talking about are the different areas of life that require just a little bit of intentional effort to reach that awful term everyone likes to throw around without even understanding what it is – balance.

TAKING GUILT OUT OF BALANCE

The term 'balance' puts guilt on the people who want to hustle and provides excuses for those who don't. That won't change until we understand what it means and how to achieve it.

All my life I have heard about the importance of becoming balanced. It appeared to be the goal of every human, although it seemed completely unrealistic to attain. Based on what I saw on TV, only gurus in robes had ever been able to reach this elite accomplishment and pass on the secrets to achieve it. I wanted to learn, grow, and be better, but I just couldn't see a path for someone like me to get there. I wasn't a guru and my old robe has holes in it. During this time, I felt that I didn't need to work less. I didn't need to work more either. I just needed to figure out this 'balance' and I would regain control of my days again. How on earth was I going to get there when I couldn't find clean socks?

Then one day, it clicked. Well, one day after years of books, podcasts and coaching:

You don't work to achieve balance. Balance is achieved by doing the work!

THE FOUR AREAS

Balance comes from growing in several areas of your life simultaneously. The best part is that the effort in each area does not need to be equal! If each area were split in a pie chart, each slice could be a different size.

Victory comes when there is awareness and intentional effort in the following four areas:

- Spiritual and Emotional
- Physical
- Personal Connections
- Financial

Since I like to keep things simple, I quickly realized that seven, nine, or twelve of anything is too much. Setting goals in just 4 Areas of Life is all that's required to create the fulfilling life you desire. I capitalize the phrase '4 Areas of Life' because to me, it's a proper noun to name a way of living.

The following examples visualize different ways to feel alignment. The percentage represents the effort you put into a single area, and may fluctuate during different seasons of life. What is imperative is that none are being neglected or put on cruise control to retirement.

4 Areas of Life

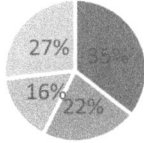

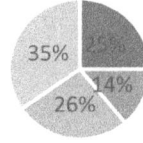

4 Areas of Life

27% 35%
16% 22%

35% 25%
14%
26%

- Financial
- Spiritual & Emotional
- Physical
- Personal Connection

- Financial
- Spiritual & Emotional
- Physical
- Personal Connection

At any given time, your personal effort in the 4 Areas of Life can be as uneven as the pie charts above, yet you still feel balanced because each area is getting the work needed for continued growth *no matter your starting point*. Mix and match to accommodate any season of life you are in, but keep all four areas in constant growth mode.

The objective is to flip from neglecting the things you assume are automatically taking care of themselves to applying the energy and awareness they deserve. Your relationship may feel stable, but are you putting in deliberate effort to prevent it from becoming stagnant or complicated? Not only does focusing on the 4 Areas of Life bring you balance, it's also a form of preventative care.

IT'S THE JOURNEY, NOT THE RESULT

You do not have to achieve perfection to be considered balanced, either. Being clear on your direction and taking small steps to get there are what gives us that feeling of alignment.

For example, you don't need to be fit to hit 'balance,' but you can't neglect the physical when you are more focused on the financial. Instead of long, body-building workouts, maybe short, mind-clearing workouts are what you need to keep working toward improvement. You can't neglect the spiritual and emotional either, but you don't need to deep dive into the meaning of life when you are in a season devoted to creating memories and deepening relationships.

While it's okay that all areas aren't equally divided, it is important each is quickly brought to a standard that matches your values. For example, if your finances are a mess, you have no idea where your money goes and you have more credit cards than Tupperware containers without lids, it's necessary that the percentage of focus in this area is higher than the others for a period of time. Once it's in alignment, you can redistribute your effort.

When we neglect any of these four areas, the cracks in our lack of planning, preparing and direction begin to show themselves over time. That's when we start to operate in survival mode and become more reactive to the damage that is done. Although things may be 'fine' now, without clear aim we are at high risk of losing something important in life down the road due to the lack of effort today.

When I discovered and implemented action within all 4 Areas of Life, the game really changed. I never needed to reduce my hours. I needed to be clearer and more deliberate about the hours worked, as well as the hours with my family. Balancing the 4 Areas of Life made everything improve, and I could see that balance reflected off of the people around me.

To those hustling and trying to build something with urgency, this doesn't mean you need to scale back your work before something crashes. Ultimate success will come by adding in the same urgency and effort into your personal life. By doing this, you will naturally revisit your priorities and design an entire life with intention. The following pages will give you the skills necessary to achieve greatness, balance, and peace and drop any guilt associated with the journey.

2

Own Your Decisions

When I was about nineteen, I made a pencil drawing of a girl. No one in particular, just a random girl. I wasn't one of those naturally gifted artists that could just pick up a pencil and make magic happen, but I had some talent that just needed more training. I was excited to expand my potential.

I spent hours on this drawing. I worked up and erased the eyes over and over until I could feel the emotion in them. I added just enough shading to make her look three-dimensional. For my first attempt at freehand, I thought it was pretty good.

My dad *is* one of those naturally gifted artists that could pick up just about any tool and turn it into a masterpiece. He was sketching realistic landscapes while his playmates drew stick figures, and he was guaranteed to win every art contest he entered. I was excited to show him what I had created. I knew it had some flaws, but expected him to tell me it was wonderful just because he was my dad and that's what he thought of anything I did.

He told me he loved the drawing, then proceeded to point out the imperfection in the girl's nose and that her shoulders were too broad. A few of the shadows faced the wrong way despite my effort. Although he shared these critiques with the utmost grace, I heard, "This really sucks, Jessie." After that, I didn't draw much. I don't blame him. The picture took a lot of time and time was something I didn't have to spare. Even though it brought me joy, I knew I would have to invest too much to become a more talented artist. I moved on from my drawing days.

About fifteen years later, on a visit with my parents, my dad randomly announced, "Boy, I really wish you had stuck with drawing. I remember you brought home a drawing of a girl and I was blown away by how good it was."

After an awkward stutter, I managed to exclaim, "But Dad, you pointed out all the things wrong with it!" He immediately, without apology, acknowledged that he had, but not because it was bad. Because he felt it was so good, if I could just fix a few things, it could have been perfect. He saw my potential, not the flaws. Looking back on that conversation, he did tell me how fantastic it was numerous times, yet I only heard comments about her nose and shoulders and created my own narrative. He was hoping to push me to another level. I heard I wasn't good enough to even play on the field.

WE HEAR WHAT WE WANT

So many times, we hear what we want to hear – or hear what we don't want to hear – regardless of what was said. Watching my older daughters play sports, I've seen their confidence become affected by what the coach doesn't say to them as often as what they do say.

When my middle daughter, Hannah, was about ten, she could get off of the field and tell me how many times her soccer coach told her she was doing a good job. "Mom! He said 'good job' four times today!" That built up her confidence. Do you know what tore it down just as quickly? When the coach told other girls they were doing a great job and didn't say anything to Hannah. This is very common in young female athletes (and females in general). When they hear someone else getting a pat on the back, they compare that to the feedback, or lack of feedback, they received. That silence sounds like "You suck" or "You're not as good" in their heads.

It is absolutely exhausting creating narratives in your head. A 'good job' is just a good job. It shouldn't put you on cloud nine for the day or cause overthinking because you wish it had been a 'great job.' These bouts of self-created ups and downs, drain important energy from the things that matter.

These narratives can follow us into areas of our life that are greater than drawing or youth soccer. When our family friend told me I was working too hard and needed to cut back, the first thing I heard was, "You aren't putting your family first. You're being selfish." He hadn't said any of that. Every comment can sting if we haven't learned to own our decisions yet. Without confidence in who we are and the path we're on, we can allow these comments to morph into something they aren't and second-guess ourselves.

For years, I let the comments of others become the judgments in my life. I desperately fought that line between what I felt was best for our family and what I had been taught a family should look like. By hearing things that were never actually said, I let outside influences dictate my belief in how well we were doing as a family unit. So much of my exhaustion was brought on by that voice in my head. Finally, I had enough. It was time to start making my own decisions and own it.

When I went back to work after my first daughter was born, a well-intentioned co-worker asked if I worried about missing her first steps. What I heard was, "You are a horrible mother who's going to miss the most important moments of your child's life, and they will never forgive you for that." That simple question turned into guilt and shame as I started questioning all of the choices I was making in my life, from the type of laundry detergent I was using, to my ambitious career goals. I took that one pretty far. Whoops.

Here is how all of my children's first steps played out. I can't tell you if I saw their first steps or not. It's not because I may or may not have been there. It's because I just don't remember all the details of that blurry, raising-toddlers, period in my life. I remember funny moments, sad moments, happy moments, and so many moments in between. I definitely remember thinking that I *needed* to remember this moment or else I'd be a bad mom, but I don't actually remember each child's first steps, how old they were, and if I was there. Great news – they don't remember either! But they do know I have been, and will always be, a constant in their life.

UNPOPULAR DECISION

I have three daughters, and at the time I write this, they are seventeen, sixteen, and seven. There's a pretty good gap between the older two and the third. (And to the stranger in the grocery store who asked if they have the same father – that is a totally inappropriate question, but yes, they do. That's a moment I vividly remember!) When my first daughter, Alexis, was born, I quickly realized the baby stage was one I struggled with. There are many women who can sit and cuddle a baby and soak up every minute. I was not one of them.

For me, I dreaded those supposedly peaceful moments. I felt anxiety as the to-do list in my head continued to grow the longer I sat. I also missed work – both the productivity and the social aspect. My husband stepped up and worked longer hours to help make up for the loss of my income, but to me, work was so much more than just the money. I am appreciative of his effort, but there were days he was frustrated with his job and wished he was home more, while I would give anything to be at the job I enjoyed. Already struggling with post-partum depression, I let jealousy and resentment take over. A dark cloud hung over me during my first six-week maternity leave. When I went back to work, within days the cloud lifted and I just felt brighter.

After Alexis was just six months old, I found out I was pregnant again. Nine months later, our second daughter, Hannah, was born. Another six weeks off, another bout of depression, resentment, and jealousy. Numerous people felt the need to let me know that having two children so close together was going to be a lot to handle and to be prepared for the lack of sleep. I bought right into their prophecy.

After the second six-week maternity leave, I returned to work slowly. Only a few hours a day, but when I was home, I felt guilty about any unfinished work and when I was at work, I felt I was missing important milestones at home. A common theme for new mothers.

Alexis and Hannah weren't difficult babies, but they did cry a lot and picked up on my emotions. When I was stressed, they were stressed. When I was happy, they were happy; I just wasn't happy a lot. I didn't know how to be during that time.

Years later, Scott really wanted a third child, but as you can imagine, I needed a little more convincing. I had been working on myself since Hannah's birth, and I was in a great place mentally. There were no more dark clouds and I couldn't be sure a baby wouldn't change that. Any sort of agreement required some tough conversations together, including one I wasn't sure he'd understand – I didn't want to take a maternity leave. There, I said it. I did not want to take any time off. I wanted to continue work as usual, and I wanted to make sure I had his support before we agreed on bringing another child into the family.

We weighed the pros and cons, laid out potential concerns, and unanimously agreed – we would try to have a third child.

I knew this decision would be controversial, requiring me to take ownership and disallow any room for doubt. It was one of those decisions that would make people feel the need to insert their thoughts and opinions, but I knew we could execute this plan in a way that would be best suited for our family if we could block out the noise.

Fortunately, I had been working remote for years and Scott is self-employed so we knew he could arrange his schedule to be home when necessary. This meant that I would continue to work each day, with breaks to feed and hold a newborn, while we brought in help daily. Clients wouldn't know there was a major life change and it was business as usual – though, some gibberish responses at three a.m. did lead to one client asking if I had a drinking problem.

While Scott was fully supportive of our plan, my company didn't know what to do with it. It made our president slightly uncomfortable as he was concerned with the perception of his support. He didn't care if I took time off or not, but there was worry his support may come across as his wanting me to work more. Human Resources had to make a few calls to ensure I was allowed to work immediately after having a baby (whaaattt?). One male executive was kind enough to ask if I was sure since I was going to need some "emotional time" (?!?!?!). After a couple weeks, I finally got the answer I was hoping for: "Sure, it's your choice. If you change your mind, let us know."

Finley joined our family in the summer of 2015, during another massive refi boom where I'd already broken my prior sales record despite only being half way through the year. In the first days, I divided my time between my new baby and responding to emails and work matters. Some may say I had my priorities wrong, or accuse me of being absent, but I can tell you with certainty that Finley was surrounded by love at all times and this allowed her to get the best of me when I did hold her.

This schedule also gave me a good amount of energy to do the things I was resentful about missing when Alexis and Hannah were born. I would hold Finley in one arm, kissing her sweet little cheeks, while talking to a client about his new mortgage. I'm not sure if I knew she was going to be my last child or I just had more confidence and emotional stability then I did after my first two, but I remember so much more about Finley and her early days. By making choices that eliminated negative emotions, I had the capacity to enjoy and remember those days, whether I was holding her or making sales calls.

When Scott and I took Finley for her one-week checkup, we shared with the doctor that I was already back working in a high-stress environment. He was an older doctor and full of experience working with parents and children, so I wasn't sure how he might respond. He looked me straight in the eyes and asked, "Are you happy?" When I said yes, he responded with, "Happy mom, happy baby." Done. There was nothing else to discuss.

And I was happy. Years later, I can still remember the feeling of fulfillment. I felt like I had broken a barrier that could give other women permission to be fantastic at whatever they want to be – even if that means choosing the opposite of what I had chosen to do! There was no dark cloud after this baby. There was no post-partum depression, anger, or jealousy.

Here's the best part. Finley was, and still is, the happiest of all three of my children. She picked up on our family demeanor at the time, which I can only describe as joyful, and she brought her own joy. I was bringing my best self to my family during her developmental years and didn't worry about missing moments. I was too busy creating new ones that best suited us. There was no guilt. There was no doing what society expected of me. I was present at work and I was present at home because both were designed to meet our family's needs.

I gained a new family motto:

Live the way I want my children to live.

When we have children, we don't want them to struggle with guilt, shame, or lack of self-confidence. Yet, we don't always take the steps necessary to overcome these feelings ourselves. The day I decided to own all of my decisions unapologetically was the day I stopped feeling guilt and regret. It's a lesson I've been able to teach my daughters, not just by my words, but by my example.

CREATING CONFIDENCE THROUGH DECISIONS

My middle daughter, Hannah, lives and breathes soccer. Alexis has always been good at multiple things, and we're still watching Finley's strengths unfold, but Hannah has found that one thing she is great at and has stuck with since we first signed her up at five years old.

When you are that young, you play one game a week and maybe have a practice or two. But when you decide you're ready for the next level, that's when things can get out of control if you let them. And boy, did we let them! As she grew and met more players and coaches, she was invited to help with more teams, participate in extra practices, and travel nationally and internationally.

When each opportunity came up, I always asked her if she wanted to play, and she always said yes. She was enthusiastic and excited and believed each touch on the ball was going to get her closer to her dreams.

She loved it – until the day she started to burn out. She's eleven years old and I could see she's tired. She longs to lay on the couch or spend time with friends, but she sighs as I tell her that her schedule says we have to leave for another game.

I wanted to fix it. I wanted to call coaches and let them know she couldn't do it. I was afraid she'd have enough and quit soccer forever. What a shame that would be. She was so good. How could I fix this? Was this my fault? To be honest, I was having as much fun watching as she was playing that I never really considered her breaking point.

Then I realized something. It's not my job to protect her from her limits. It's my job to navigate her through what saying yes to everything would look like and to teach her to make adjustments for the next season. She needed to learn to say yes or no, and embrace her decisions without apology. She needed these lessons to find the balance between getting better and also taking care of herself.

It's her responsibility to explore her limits while learning how to assess and reassess, reflect and reinvent her choices. These discoveries are where our self-confidence comes from – both in children and adults. Every time we overcome adversity, we grow stronger and more trusting in ourselves and our decision-making. Why prevent the ones we love from experiencing and overcoming obstacles to gain their own self-confidence?

The first year of Hannah learning to say no was tough. If she had to decide between two different activities on the same evening, she would ask me what she should do. Attempting to push the decision back on her, I would ask questions about what she wanted, what was more fun or challenging (whichever she needed at the time), and what would get her closer to her goal. This helped her pick one, but then she immediately asked if that was the right decision. Next, she would second-guess herself and pick the other. Finally, she would start to panic and we would start all over.

It's taken her a long time to acquire the necessary skills, but as she gets older and the stakes get higher, her ability to weigh the pros and cons, assess her body and her goals, and commit to a decision has also increased. She has learned to trust herself while making judgments based on the information she has at that time. This has caused her confidence to skyrocket. Our household mantra has become *decide, own it, and move on.*

Are you able to do the same? If you have a job offer to consider, can you be decisive, or does it eat at you until you've second-guessed yourself out of anything exciting, new or thrilling in your life?

When you make a decision, do you find yourself justifying it to your audience? There's nothing wrong with listening to feedback, but don't confuse a constructive viewpoint with someone who is fixated on their way of doing things.

"Indecision is the thief of opportunity."

—Jim Rohn

LET OTHERS DECIDE

Don't create adversity and trying times – there will be plenty that come on their own – but don't prevent them from happening to yourself or others. I am now thankful I didn't see Hannah's burnout coming. College commitments are on the horizon for both of my older daughters, but I am confident they now have the skills to make the best decisions for themselves.

Working through maternity leave is not for everyone, and I would never offer that as advice. However, I hope my choice will give you the permission to determine what is best for you in any situation and own it. You may miss moments, but when you make the best choice from your best self, the moments you do create will come with joy instead of burden.

One of the reasons it was so hard to make my maternity decision was because I was worried about what Scott would say. Not because he wouldn't have been supportive, but because the way society says things must be done is so ingrained in us, I wasn't sure if he realized skipping maternity leave was an option.

I recently asked Scott about the most controversial decision he has had to make. Despite his many difficult decisions, there were none he had ever considered controversial. He's never worried about what random strangers would say about the things he chose to do or what input the Human Resources department would have on his life. Not just because he owns his decisions already, but because most people don't ask him the same questions or have the same expectations of him.

We need to be supportive of everyone in our lives. We won't always know why people choose their path, nor do we need to. Their decisions may be based on security, fear, their upbringing, etc., and their choice may be significantly different than anything we would want in our life. We need to trust that others are capable of making good decisions, or recovering from bad ones, instead of judging the differences. The more support we demonstrate, the more we give people permission and confidence to trust themselves.

3

HUSTLE VS REFLECTION

"I'm going to work forever. I love what I do and I can't imagine ever not doing it."

Said my twenty-eight-year-old self to a room full of people kind enough to keep their chuckles to themselves. I sounded like Buddy the Elf hopped up on syrup. Well, fifteen years later I have the choice between calling clients or writing, and since you are reading this, you can guess which one I've chosen. I still enjoy working with clients and have a pretty involved career in several aspects of real estate, but I no longer want to bury myself in the same work all day, every day.

My priorities have shifted and I've entered a new stage of hustle where I have reduced my work effort to pursue ventures that are more meaningful. Mortgage work is still meaningful, but it's no longer the *only* work that is. During this current stage, I'm constantly looking for new things that provide energy and fulfillment, giving each activity more consideration based on internal factors, rather than external. I still learn what I can in my industry, but I've expanded my learning to new and intriguing opportunities. I love getting sucked into a new project that I can't get enough of, becoming lost in the flow of adrenaline.

That's when I learned there are two stages of life –

HUSTLE AND REFLECTION.

Despite it being the busiest time in our lives as we potentially start a family or begin new endeavors, the hustling stage is also the time when we strive to establish ourselves and build the life we envisioned in our youth. It usually takes place early in life while time feels plenty and energy is abundant. Or, as my editor put it, "We may have more time and energy, but we don't always feel it." I can't argue with that.

The latter stage is known as reflective, where we not only adjust our efforts and priorities, but also begin to evolve in a lot of our own beliefs as we gain wisdom and experience. The flip from hustle to reflection can happen at any time in one's life, but it tends to take place in the forty- to fifty-year-old range. Maybe mistakes were made during the hustle period, or maybe there wasn't much hustle at all and we need to make up for lost time. Divorce may be another reason we step into reflection, as well as burnout or health concerns. It can take a life change, or threat of change, to start the transition, or it can just happen naturally as we age.

Eventually, when we get to the reflective stage, we begin to ask ourselves if we are on the right track. How is our body holding up? Are our relationships strong? Could we retire comfortably? By following the advice in the next few chapters, you'll be able to confidently answer YES!

HOW DID YOU GET HERE?

I have been involved in several thousand real estate transactions over the years, many of them refinances. At least once a week I speak to someone saying the words, "I don't know how we got here." Their voice, quivering and full of despair, breaks my heart.

These individuals have entered the reflective years with plans to retire, but are not in the position they thought they'd be. Instead, they are needing to refinance their mortgage to pay off tens of thousands of dollars in debt. This includes a high car payment or two, credit cards balances that never seem to go down, unexpected medical bills, student loans and more. I do my best to better their situation and turn all those payments into one lower payment, but I always wonder if I truly helped them at all.

Too many times these clients have already paid on their home for ten years or more, but instead of only having twenty years left on their mortgage, they feel forced to use all their equity to consolidate their debt – which raises their payment and the majority choose to start over on a thirty-year loan. For many, this happens again and again. Without changing their spending habits; they're pressured to bury their mistakes into their mortgage.

Other clients head into retirement comfortably even with a loan on their home. The concern is not the mortgage payment. It's the additional debt ballooning out of control with no plan to eliminate. I've watched people finance guitars and pets while they were already drowning in other monthly obligations.

At what point do you stop accumulating debt and start paying it off? When do you start saying no to things you can't afford or things that force you into another monthly payment? Without a cutoff date or a detailed plan in place, there will be no change. If you think because you are in your twenties or thirties that you have plenty of time to figure it out – you don't. You'll end up with plenty of time cementing bad spending habits and accumulate more high interest debt if you don't have a plan for your money *today*.

You say once your car is paid off, you will be debt free? Awesome. Have you started planning for your next vehicle? If you don't manage debt, debt will manage you. You can make it disappear into another loan, but if you don't change your habits, the debt will continue reappearing – and you'll still have that other loan.

When I refinance people for this purpose, I'm fully aware the root of the problem lingers. After the consolidation, I encourage them to put the savings into an emergency fund to avoid financing their next expense. The hope is that using cash will force them to consider how bad they even want that guitar or pet. Sadly, in a few years, I know many will be back to refinance all the new liabilities and start over with a new thirty-year term. And with no guarantee the equity will be there the next time around, this isn't a sustainable option.

Not all debt is bad; however, if you are broke, struggling, or making great money that keeps disappearing, adding to your monthly obligations isn't the solution. Aimlessly collecting and spending money will cause you to wake up one day and wonder where it went or how you got here – just like many of my clients. On the flip side, if you create a plan for your spending and execute it in alignment with your financial values, you'll find yourself in the reflective stage relaxing in the financial position you had hoped.

To retire with very little debt, or none at all, what steps do you need to take today?

The answer: Hustle. (Wait…keep reading!)

DEFINING HUSTLE

You may be thinking that hustle means longer hours, never saying no to an extra shift, or giving up weekends, but that's not it at all. Working more hours may be the answer depending on your situation, but when I talk about hustling, I'm talking about more than just making money. Finances are only one of the 4 Areas of Life that you need to hustle in early on so you can enjoy your reflective years later.

Hustling is about being as uncomfortable as you can in your high energy season so you feel as peaceful as possible in your reflective years.

Webster's defines hustle as: to push, crowd, or force forward roughly; to move or work rapidly and tirelessly.

No wonder hustle has become a word so many want to avoid. We don't want to be perceived as forcing forward or working tirelessly; it doesn't sound like a fulfilling life. But if we apply this mindset to all 4 Areas of Life – spiritual and emotional, physical, personal connections, and financial – we can turn hustle into our life raft.

We have all heard stories of an employee who never made more than $50,000 a year in their entire career, yet retired a millionaire. How does that happen? Because they hustled. They defined their values and worked toward their goals like there was no other option. Their hustle didn't come in the form of more employment hours, yet they still worked rapidly and tirelessly with sacrifice and discipline.

If the reflective stage is so critical in our lives, why are we so nonchalant about getting there? We allow ourselves to be indifferent about how we retire, what impact we leave on this earth, and how we feel about others. Hustle isn't limited to work ethic. While many engage in mediocre work during the few hours they do show up, their relationships are also mundane, their finances are questionable, and their emotions are as controlled as a kid in a candy store. How do you think that will play out in the reflective years?

WAKING UP

When I really started focusing on growing my business the same time as my first refinance boom – I was a mess. 'Trainwreck' was the word I used to refer to myself. My days were out of control and there were constant fires and issues erupting that I was just reacting to. Stress emanated from my body as I walked into a room. Even in the calm, I was tense and anxious waiting for the next explosion. I didn't even want to be around myself; I can't even imagine what others thought when they saw me coming.

My kids could feel this stress too, I could see it on their faces. It made sense that someone advised me to work less, but it wouldn't have made a difference. Who I was needed to change, not what I was doing. If I quit an hour earlier every day, that just meant everyone had to spend an extra hour with me. That definitely wasn't the solution. I knew something was broke and needed fixing, but I couldn't articulate what it was. I had numerous co-workers whose work issues mirrored mine, yet I was the one gasping for air.

Luckily, this was the time I met my first life coach. When she asked what I hoped to accomplish, I explained the chaos in my head and lack of time management, but I was clear – there was nothing I was willing to give up. Good luck, I thought. This lady has no idea what she's in for.

As she dug in, I learned a lot. First, I despise personality tests. Who cares if I'm a lion or part penguin and ostrich!? But more importantly, I learned I had to reassess my morning routine. When my coach asked me to tell her about my day, I didn't even get to 'brushing my teeth' before she solved most of my problems.

Every morning, after hitting snooze too many times, I would finally jump out of bed and start yelling at Alexis and Hannah to wake up. When they wouldn't move right away, I'd yell louder. I must have assumed they couldn't hear me. Since they took more than the one minute allotted for them to wake up, that put all the other tasks behind and we had to sacrifice things like eating breakfast in order to make it out the door on time. Inevitably, someone always lost a shoe. By the time we got out the door, everyone was in tears. Then I jumped straight into emails, never giving my blood pressure a break.

The advice from my coach was simple. Wake up thirty minutes early tomorrow. If I need to hit snooze four times, set the alarm accordingly. I couldn't find an excuse to fight it, so I gave it a shot. With this extra time, I was able to gently wake the girls. They didn't get up on my first attempt, but there was enough time to keep trying without the screaming. Those extra minutes allowed everyone to calmly get dressed and eat breakfast. And somehow that extra time caused the second shoe to appear!

Our house went from dread to joy each morning. The stress, anxiety, and yelling disappeared. We even added the luxury of a few laughs before the day started. We continued to get up earlier and add to our routine, and with everyone enjoying the morning now, Alexis and Hannah started getting up on their own.

WAKING UP…AGAIN…EARLIER?

A few years later, I worked with a small group who were all about personal growth and development. They decided to commit to getting up one hour earlier than their current schedule and asked me to join their self-inflicted agony. Everyone would start with the time they normally wake up and set their alarm an hour earlier, texting the group for accountability. Texts rolled in between 4 a.m. to 8 a.m. and to this day, I wake up at five in the morning. As exhausting as the new habit was, it led to another transformation. Having someone hold me accountable was key.

My earlier hours allowed me to add extra activities that I call 'the disciplines' and will share in more detail later. The great thing about the disciplines is that you can choose as few or as many of the ones you feel are best for you. It's just about adding small tasks to your life that will lead to large gains. Mine include:

Journaling – Whether it's goal setting, reflecting on my day, laying out my future self, or sharing my struggles, I take a little time to write out where my head is and where it needs to be. There are periods of mindless drivel, but by sticking with it, eventually, I'll get my groove back.

Reading – I read a few pages of a personal development book each morning. I love biographies also, but I save those for extra reading time or audio books. The morning is about personal growth and I never finish a book I can't connect with. (Yikes! I see the irony of the advice potentially causing you to put this book down. Hopefully you'll keep going.)

Meditating – Although I've been known to fall asleep during meditation, even just five to ten minutes of silence and listening each morning can be life altering. That decision you've been fretting over? The answer may clearly reveal itself during this time.

Working out – Even a few minutes to get the blood flowing produces a boost of energy. Some days, it's only a short workout in the morning. Others, it's about building strength and confidence. Even an abbreviated work-out will get the heartrate up and head cleared!

~ ~ ~

These four things don't take a lot of time and effort. They are personal to me, so no one can tell me if I'm doing them right or wrong. Falling asleep during mediating likely isn't recommended by the experts, but I'm getting better and out-hustling those who stay comfortable.

Not only has this routine given me that balance that everyone says we need, it's given me peace. It's fulfilling to my family mission – *to live the way I want my children to live.*

Getting up earlier has had such an impact, all of my children now wake with ample time to have their own routines. As a matter of fact, Hannah took this to an extreme. She started getting up over two hours before she needed to leave for school to watch TV. It was unnecessary and cutting into my quiet time. I had to set limits on how early she could leave her bed! Although she sleeps a little longer now, Hannah's morning demeanor is contagious. She is Zen-like and calm, which came from my choice to hustle.

WHEN YOU GROW – EVERYTHING GROWS

I didn't cut my hours, I added more to my routine. I worked harder – on myself. When I did start looking at emails and talking to clients, my body was calm and my head was clear.

My business began to grow because I was growing with it. When the fires came, they were no longer dramatic episodes. They were extinguished quickly and quietly since I had widened my mental and emotional capacity. I could build better relationships with clients, but most importantly, I became a better mother, wife, and human.

I learned that there's nothing wrong with working hard, as long as you can do it without negatively impacting others. There's nothing wrong with hustling. It's respectable to spend your high-energy years building so you can spend your reflective years unwinding.

Now that I've entered my reflective season, I look back proud of what I've accomplished. Not just in accolades, but in the lessons I have learned and passed on to my daughters. As a family, we experienced hardships and tears through the hustling years, but that discomfort has made us stronger and put us on a sturdy foundation.

Just by being aware of the 4 Areas of Life and working toward a better self in each area, I gain as much peace in the journey as if I had already received the results. In the next chapters, I am going to share with you how you can find peace and balance in your life without sacrificing that which you wish to accomplish, no matter the season of life you are in.

PART TWO

THE FOUR AREAS OF LIFE

Spiritual and Emotional

Physical

Personal Connections

Financial

4

AREA ONE:
SPIRITUAL AND EMOTIONAL

Since all areas are equally important, starting with the spiritual and emotional has no special significance. They all require awareness and effort, and you can determine which gets the higher percentage based on your personal needs and the amount of work that needs to be done.

I've combined both spiritual and emotional into a single category for two reasons. First, I believe you can't have one without the other. If you target growth in one, you will automatically develop in both. Second, working in four important areas of your life is much easier than five. I'm all about easier.

This belief wasn't always the case for me, though. Growing up, everything I learned about the spiritual and emotional was tied to religion. There were rules to follow and beliefs to believe. The very structured plan laid out a specific gateway to Heaven and how to create a relationship with God. This relationship was one based on fear.

I grew up in a small Baptist church. The leadership made it clear that we were not to question God, the Bible, or their interpretation of either. If you did have doubts, the pastor was equipped to tell you all the reasons this church had the one and only truth. I understood we were all sinners, but the list of sins to avoid was pretty daunting, especially to an awkward teenager who spent her time angry, annoyed, and sneaking rock music into her Sony Walkman. I lived in constant fear, guilt and shame of the thoughts flowing through my head. Oh, and there was no way I would doubt any of this either; that was a sin. Constantly reminded how lucky I was to have the answers, I spent most of my teenage years in confusion. There were things I didn't have the capacity to comprehend at that age, and even today, I'm still scratching my head.

ALLOW CURIOSITY

As I got older, I started to understand that curiosity and questions are how you learn and grow. Due to the fear, it took years before I would find the courage to begin to question the "one and only truth." I am not saying these truths were wrong or right; I am just saying I finally had the confidence to examine them for myself. Once I did, I learned quickly that actively seeking the answers for yourself can lead to just as much peace as having the answers you're searching for.

It's important to allow others to seek their truth too. Your personal and spiritual beliefs are exactly that – personal. They don't have to be hidden, but adamantly insisting that your way is right stifles others from pursuing their journey and obtaining the answers they need to find. Scaring someone into believing as you do doesn't allow a genuine relationship with whomever or whatever you hope they believe in. No one wins.

About four years ago, I was having a fantastic conversation about religion with someone I had just met. (That sentence made many people cringe; I know.) Most follow the rule not to speak about religion, especially with new acquaintances, but I was sure this was different. We appeared to have a connection, and within our twenty-minute friendship, we found ourselves talking about all sorts of deep topics. I pictured us sharing best-friend necklaces in no time! Then, when a prevalent belief regarding the Christian faith came up, I simply explained that, although I'm open-minded, I don't understand it well enough to agree. To which my new best friend replied, "You're wrong."

Wait, what?! We just spent the last twenty minutes discussing my upbringing and commitment to rebuilding my spiritual beliefs and your response is, "You're wrong!" Needless to say, I never purchased that best-friend necklace. I was open and excited to discuss why she believed what she did, but I can no longer believe something just because someone told me to.

True growth means that sometimes we have more questions than answers on the things we thought we already knew. We reexamine the guidance taught to us when we were children. We revisit our relationship with family, money, politics, and God – even things we were taught not to question, or never considered questioning before.

Does this make our parents, or other influences in our young life wrong? Absolutely not. They likely took the same journey to determine what was right and wrong and best for us at the time.

I have never denied any of what I have been taught. I have just decided to strip the 'believe it or else' preachings from my life and take my own spiritual journey. For me, starting over meant I had to remove all religious teachings and get back to basics. That may not be the case for you, but don't be afraid to add or remove what's necessary in your life to continue to be open-minded.

Still searching for answers, I continue asking the questions needed to fulfill my journey. It's an active search that allows me to feel balanced, yet never complacent. I'm not ready to settle for the knowledge I have at this time, so I will keep researching, at peace with my efforts.

The growth in our spiritual and emotional journey can be endless. No matter the peak we reach, there is always another mountain to climb. How we pursue the truth, and the path we take, will vary person to person, but the target remains the same – understanding our purpose and achieving maximum potential in our lives. I personally lean more heavily on trying to understand what a relationship with God looks like because of the foundation that was laid during my youth. Your spiritual journey may be geared towards connecting with the Universe daily to be guided through your time on Earth. Or, your pursuit may be feeling and controlling your emotions in order to achieve a higher level of self-awareness.

START FROM THE BEGINNING

My first step was stripping away everything I was told, even what I believed to be true. I remember debates in our church over whether God, Jesus, and the Holy Ghost were separate or one in the same. When I decided to start over, I realized the answer was completely irrelevant to my current journey. They were exciting topics for the adults to engage in, but had no bearing on what it meant to their faith. When I removed all of that noise, I realized much of the ideology discussed wasn't going to impact my current life or afterlife. I had been chasing answers to questions that some may find fun to explore, but right then, they weren't necessary and caused needless confusion. I had to truly start at zero.

After removing twenty-plus years of noise and skepticism, I determined the next step required me to shut up and listen. Despite being unsure of what I would find, I turned to meditation. The exercise wasn't easy at first. I would get distracted and start planning my lunches instead of listening to whatever it was I was supposed to hear.

But out of that initial mess, positive results began to emerge. I started to clearly feel my emotions and why they were presenting themselves. As thoughts came and went, I could identify anxiety, jealousy, bitterness, and more. By recognizing these emotions in the quiet of my day, I gained the skills to identify and conquer them when they came up in the middle of the chaos. When my heart started racing and I began to feel overwhelmed, I could immediately diagnose the cause and make the necessary mindset adjustment.

While meditation definitely helped me connect with myself, it also helped me connect more deeply to whatever else was out there. I started getting answers to questions I wasn't even asking! This allowed me to determine which beliefs felt right and why they made sense. I watched truths unfold right in front of me.

This revelation changed my feelings regarding prayer. When I was growing up, every prayer needed to start with a greeting like *Dear*

Heavenly Father and end with an *Amen*. If not, was it even a prayer? In between, we included a lot of *thank you for this*, *forgive me for that*, *heal them*, and *can I please have…* (hey, ask and ye shall receive!). It was pretty scripted, boring, and formal. When I turned to meditation, my connection became more real and authentic. The Universe, God, or whatever you meditate to doesn't respond because you started with a proper greeting. The response comes through your attempts to get aligned to communicate.

No matter whom or what you seek, you can connect by just listening.

Regardless of how you were brought up, there will come a point in your life when you will question its purpose, meaning, and your place in it. Meditation will help you find calm and clarity in the middle of the hustle and provide you answers and connections to lift you to another level in your life. Maybe you sought this activity initially to connect with a higher power, but in turn, it guided you to a legacy you had never considered for yourself. Meditation will provide you with what you need, as well as what you didn't know you needed, as you quietly allow thoughts to flow through you.

BELIEVE IN SOMETHING BIGGER THAN YOURSELF

Now I'm going to do my best to follow my own advice. I am trying not to tell you what to believe in, but that being said, life makes more sense when you believe in something bigger than yourself. Maybe it's an emotion like love, or an all-being power like God. It may be the Universe or the Church. You might even see all of those as the same. In any case, life has more meaning when it doesn't revolve around you. Why? Because it doesn't.

There are over seven billion of us on this planet. How can we all be the most important person on Earth? Making myself the center of my own universe is a surefire way to suddenly lose clarity and purpose in what I'm trying to accomplish. When I acknowledge my existence revolves around a higher power and purpose, overcoming mistakes and obstacles become easier, and paths begin to unfold that I hadn't seen before.

Your bigger belief may be your family. Knowing your spouse is expecting you to give 100% while you're away is enough to push you to be your best self. Knowing your children are watching may be another motivator. Setting the example to live life to the fullest can be a driving force for you day in and day out. Though all great inspiration, what happens if something changes in the family dynamic? What will drive you then? What will hold you together? Believing in something bigger than ourselves means believing in something bigger than any other human. Something that can't be destroyed.

HIGHEST BELIEF

This leads to the highest belief you can hold. Have you ever played the 'I love you more' game with a child or loved one? One starts with I love you and the response is 'I love you more.' Then it escalates with 'love you to the moon and back' and 'infinity and beyond.' Finley and I have played this, and once I hit infinity, she will try to trump me. I have explained to her that there is nothing greater than infinity, but she refuses to lose.

What is the one belief that is the greatest of all your beliefs? It could never be destroyed. It's the belief that takes you to infinity and beyond and calls to you for continuous growth. There are so many books that talk about your 'why', and you should read each and every one of them, but I want you to think even bigger. Having a why only goes so far. Why did I set such high goals in 2013? Yes, I wanted to make money, but my why was to put us in a better financial position so we wouldn't have to worry about the bad times. Growing up, there were times we had money and times there was nothing. It was imperative we were prepared for the latter.

But this why could only get me so far. Once I felt pretty good about our financial position, I became stuck. My why no longer drove me when I weighed the obstacles in my career. It no longer excited me enough to try new things and take calculated risks. I needed a bigger reason to keep making this effort.

I needed my highest belief to push me. I had to ask myself what I felt my purpose for being on the Earth was. More than my family, more than my career. What pushes me to be my best self each and every day? Keeping my highest belief in the forefront keeps my brain energized and developing creative thoughts. It keeps me ready for the next opportunity or idea that I haven't yet imagined.

Every time I need to reinvent myself or feel I've lost my way, I connect to my highest belief, and find the answer that is going to excite and propel me into a new adventure. Even days I think I'm clear about my direction, I still like to check in to ensure I am still where I need to be and am growing in all 4 Areas of Life.

FINDING YOUR HIGHEST BELIEF

You may have never considered how your highest belief impacts your goals or purpose, even in the smallest areas. Or, you may have complete certainty about your purpose in connection with that belief. Either way, the following questions can help you understand your highest belief or deepen your relationship with it. This exercise also ensures you don't lose yourself or your values while you are chasing big dreams and goals.

- What are the most important things on this Earth to me?
- If I were to lose any of these things tomorrow, what would keep me going?
- *Besides family*, what inspires me to get better each and every day?
- What are the ways I feel reassured I'm on the right path?
- When I listen to myself, what am I listening for?
- Do I trust my own inner voice? Why or why not?
- What are three beliefs I was taught in my youth? (May include spiritual, emotional, financial, etc.; i.e., *big girls don't cry* or *only expensive cars are safe cars*)
- How have these beliefs changed over the years?
- Have my childhood beliefs limited or excelled me? How so?
- There are over 7 billion people on this Earth – why have I been made one of them?

- Our time on Earth is limited. What must I accomplish to fulfill my purpose?
- Why do these accomplishments matter to me?

Assess, reassess, and dig deep within yourself until you discover your highest belief – stronger than any goal, vision or why. Focusing on just one question a day will allow greater reflection before you move on to the next.

EMOTIONAL INTELLIGENCE

While the spotlight to this point has been on the spiritual, emotional growth may be more of an interest, or more of a need to you right now. Lacking in emotional intelligence may be causing a rift in your life. Perhaps your relationship is suffering because your time is spent in anger or hurt that you can't let go of. Maybe your work is stagnant as you engulf yourself in frustration or despair. You may feel it's always everyone else's fault, though. You wouldn't be hurt if others respected you. You would get that promotion if your office wasn't full of drama or people trying to sabotage your efforts.

A few weeks after we moved, Alexis had a sleepover. She invited only four girls from her softball team, leaving twelve off the guest list. She had just recently joined this team, so she didn't know many of the girls, and she didn't want the responsibility of hosting a large gathering. We didn't consider it to be a team event, just a small get together. I invited the parents of the girls to stay for dinner as each one was dropped off.

A few days later, I received a nervous call from one of the mothers who had stayed with her daughter. She apologized for bothering me, but she had been losing sleep over what she was about to tell me, and felt I needed to know that I was going to get confronted. "Confronted for what?" I asked. She went on to explain that an uninvited parent was under the impression that this was a team gathering and that the oversight was intentional. Neither accusation was accurate.

The angered mom had been calling the invited mom all week, shaming her for going to this 'party' and not telling her about it, as well as not bringing her daughter. I learned that this parent had been bad-mouthing me to other parents, including those not part of the team.

I thanked the mom for telling me and assured her I'd be fine. But before I could get off the phone, I felt the conversation wasn't over. Feeling her confusion, I checked on her, "Are you okay?" For the next few minutes, this mother proceeded to tell me how distraught she was. She had lost sleep as her "friend" had been saying awful things to her. She couldn't understand how I could be fine. I was the culprit who'd hosted the sleepover. My name had been smeared through the mud for days without my knowledge. How was I not feeling the same hell she had been?

"Simple," I responded, "All of this sounds like her problem, not mine. Drama is how you feel about something that happens – not the thing that happens. You and I are both facing the same backlash, yet we each *chose* opposite responses. It's only drama when you allow it to be. I don't feel the need to get involved."

There would have been a day I would have been just as worked up, immediately calling friends for their support, interrupting their day with my immature reactions. I'd hope they'd tell me I'd done nothing wrong, instead of being confident enough in my own abilities to assess my behavior and apologize when required.

I no longer look at another person and accuse them of creating drama. I instead look at myself and ask how I engage in the situations that present themselves. There are times my reflection reveals I let my emotions slip and escalated the situation. I need to do better. There are others when it rolls right by me without a second thought.

Emotional control grows with the ability to trust yourself. I knew I didn't have to worry about an angered mom who would possibly confront me at the next game. If she had concerns, I would kindly address them. I ran through best- and worst-case scenarios in my head and knew I was capable of handling all of them.

If you are curious, I had no intention of confronting the angry mother for the things that were being said about me. Anyone who engaged in this gossip was not someone I felt the need to defend myself to. Those who knew me could make their own assessment.

Growing your emotional intelligence takes practice. I don't consider any of my emotions a failure as they arise. Anger will still step on calm's head to make its way to the top any chance it gets. There's nothing wrong with anger; it can be a great tool to catapult me into action. Other times, I kick anger to the curb if it doesn't serve my goals and flip it until I find an emotion that does.

As I work on these emotions each and every day, they lead to a greater awareness of who I am, what I want, and how to get there. I drop the emotions that create noise and swap them for the ones that create calm, flipping through them like a Rolodex. And since two emotions can't occupy the same space at the same time, by controlling which emotion I allow in, I leave room to remain connected to what the universe has for me, not fighting with softball moms about sleepovers.

This openness in my emotional state is what connects the emotion to the spiritual. When we are caught up in the roller coaster of feelings, we can't hear our own voice or follow directions with clarity. Keeping anger, desire for vengeance, and blame in check, gives us more energy to connect with our highest belief.

It also allows more room for the things that are most meaningful to us.

PUTTING IN PRACTICE

There are numerous ways to grow in both your emotional intelligence and your spiritual journey. Be prepared to give yourself grace as you practice listening to yourself and managing the thoughts and feelings that pass through you. A lot of grace. Don't be bothered by the emotions that come up. Just don't linger on anything that doesn't serve you.

When I was hurt by a situation at work, I decided I needed a little time being angry. I tried to ignore it at first, but it kept consuming me at the wrong times each day. I finally embraced it and allowed one hour every day to plot my revenge, prepare the perfect 'I Quit' speech and think of clever comebacks in my head. After the hour was up, I was back to focusing on my future and using that anger as fuel. Eventually, being angry got tiresome and even stopped floating to the surface.

Just like any goal, these practices require specific and measurable timelines. When I journal to clear my head, I commit five days a week for at least twenty minutes a day. When I practice gratitude, I give it at least fifteen minutes to let it really soak in and last longer.

No matter your focus, constant, disciplined action will help you find a deeper, more meaningful connection to your spiritual and emotional being and to others in your life. Empathy will grow and calm will set in. Your relationships will feel the difference and your business will grow as you approach it with more intention. Your hustle won't decrease; however, your ability to achieve greatness will expand in ways you couldn't have envisioned for yourself. Imagine everything in your life reaching new levels because you added ten minutes of a new activity each day.

Once you understand your mind and body on a deeper level, you'll better grasp the importance of the upcoming areas and how to approach each deliberately. As each of the 4 Areas of Life are added into your routine, you will feel a sense of peace and balance, well before the results are obtained. Knowing you are on the right path will lead to a transformation in your life and an energy others will see in you.

5

AREA TWO:
PHYSICAL

You can have the most amazing things in life, but none of it matters if you don't have the stamina to enjoy them. Giving the best of you means more than just being in the room. Your family and friends may love simply having you in their presence, but bringing your *best* involves having the energy to participate, and showing them what living their best life should look like.

I've met some extremely successful people who struggle to walk up a flight of steps. Their breath quickly becomes short and their knees begin to falter, but they are a top producer, drive a nice car, and have a loving family. Three out of four ain't bad, but imagine having all four. Faster movement and more energy on top of an already driven mind and blessed life? Now that's an unstoppable force.

I understand society's concern when it comes to judging people's weight or health without knowing their history. Perhaps you read that last paragraph and felt appalled or offended that I would talk about someone's health without knowing all the facts, but according to the U.S. Department of Health and Human Services, nearly 1 in 3 adults (30.7%) were considered overweight in the data gathered in

2017-2018. There is a health epidemic, and it sounds like a third of us can benefit from taking better care of ourselves.

The reality is that no matter one's size or health history, there are habits we all must partake in to maintain good health. The first is to love and accept our bodies as they are. Loving them gives us the best reason to take better care of them, providing them what they need to last as long as possible with the least number of complications.

I am aware that for some, the health problems came first, limiting the physical activity or endurance. But for the rest, a large portion of heart disease, mobility issues, and diabetes originated from our own habits. We mix excessive junk and processed food with low movement and activity, producing a society full of medication for depression and anxiety, much of which (not all, I know) can be cured with exercise and a focus on mental health.

START WITH SUGAR

I was a sugar eater. I loved all snacks, ice cream and candy (still do). When Alexis was three, she asked Scott for a donut. He laughed and challenged her, "Sure, if you can find a donut, you can have it." She walked into my office, climbed on my desk, reached behind a pile of books and pulled out a bag of mini donuts. Busted.

I'm not even sure how to relate to someone who tells me they don't like sweets. What!? Really? We can't be friends. I've always just accepted sugar as part of life. Maybe I don't need to devour multiple cupcakes at a time, but I couldn't fathom a life where I would turn one down if it was presented to me.

When we went out to eat, it didn't matter how full I was, I always ordered the dessert. Has anyone been born with enough willpower to say no to a warm lava chocolate cake with vanilla ice cream? It sounds a little dramatic, but I want you to understand the magnitude of my next move.

I cut sugar.

I completely eliminated it from my diet for ninety days. It started when I was watching a Netflix documentary about sugar. I don't remember which one it was, but it conveyed the usual message about sugar being a drug and the human addiction to it.

When the documentary touched on marketing the sugary products to children and the industry making deals to put their profits ahead of our health, something clicked in me. Maybe I was angered that businesses were marketing their drugs directly to me and I was stupid enough to fall for it, or maybe I was ashamed that I hadn't eaten dinner the night before because I had two pieces of Dairy Queen ice cream cake instead. Either way, I knew in that moment I needed to make a change.

Yes, you read that right. As an adult, instead of dinner, I ate multiple pieces of Dairy Queen ice cream cake and left no room for a healthy meal. When I became winded walking up steps, it was 100% my fault. I had no genetics or childhood trauma to blame. I stuffed multiple pieces of cake in my face because, well, I liked it. I can tell you this was not the life I wanted my children to live.

During this documentary, I looked at my husband and naively exclaimed, "I'm quitting sugar for ninety days!" His jaw dropped. He enjoys eating healthy and taking care of himself, but he knew giving up sugar would be way out of my element. Although I've expanded my palate, even in adulthood I am a picky eater, so ninety days of sugar-free meals would be limiting. Scott finally responded with, "That's great. I'll help you, but just so you know, everything has sugar in it."

Next thing you know, we were huddled by the refrigerator reading nutrition labels. Five grams of sugar in our bread! I had no idea there was sugar in bread! I assumed cakes and sweets were the culprits. Yep, this was going to be hard. My favorite bread was out.

THE NEXT NINETY

The next ninety days were a nightmare mixed with the greatest experiment of my health. I spent way too much time on Google trying to plan meals and snacks in advance. To keep some of my sanity, I allowed myself to eat natural sugars, such as fruits and vegetables, and still permitted dressings and condiments. If I was going to give up all snacks for a salad, I still needed a little joy on that lettuce.

That's the great thing about setting your own goals – you can make your own exceptions. One person accused me of cheating when I used ketchup. I reminded them the alternative was going back to cake for dinner. Since I made the rules, there was no such thing as cheating.

When someone is working on bettering themselves, let's stop pointing out what we think are weaknesses. Celebrate their victories. I made gains and improvements during this time that have inspired future goals and growth, not just in myself, but in others.

Just days into the sugar-free challenge, there was a change in my body. I had more energy! I didn't feel sluggish during the workday. I slept better. And here's the kicker: every month, previous to this, I would get a little, um, moody for a few days (moody was the kind way of saying it). Not only that, but for twenty-four hours I would feel depressed and even have dark and unhealthy thoughts. These symptoms signaled my period would be starting in the next couple of days.

A couple of weeks into the ninety-day period, I walked out of the bathroom in amazement and asked Scott, "Did you know my period was starting?" He does not track these things, but based on my obvious, consistent symptoms, he usually has a pretty good idea. He looked just as stunned. Neither of us could believe there wasn't a single symptom. No change in mood, no unexplainable emotions, and most importantly, no dark thoughts.

You may think this was a fluke; however, this happened twice more during that ninety-day period. After the three months were up and I went back to sugar, I also went back to having my previous symptoms. This experiment showed me first-hand how large a role excessive sugar plays in our emotional state and our energy.

I couldn't sustain cutting sugar completely for any longer, despite the benefits. I tried to eliminate it to such an extreme that in moments of weakness, I would overcompensate and become ill. You can't avoid sugar for three weeks then devour a milkshake. My body rejected this new enemy. Research recommended that a woman my age and size could enjoy twenty- to twenty-five grams of sugar daily. That's much more tolerable for me, so one of my goals is to limit my sugar intake to twenty grams a day, at least five days a week. This meant I got to keep my favorite bread for breakfast each morning!

While striving for unattainable goals excites me in my career, I knew I needed feasible ones when it comes to my health. Five days a week marks an immense improvement from annihilating Dairy Queen ice cream for dinner, and I could grow into seven days over time. If I started with seven, I set myself up for frustration caused by failure, as well as shame or guilt from saying yes – or no – to the opportunities to indulge from time to time.

Limiting the sugar to twenty grams most days a week still gives me the energy I need, improves my skin and also keeps emotions in balance. I'm sure the unseen, long-term health benefits are the real winner.

EXERCISE

While cutting unhealthy foods helps, rounding out the physical area is exercise. A no-brainer to many, and I'm not sure I can add much more than you already know, but much like the sugar, I leave room for improvement.

I have a lot of respect for the person who can cut out all sugar. That's great, but that's not me, at least not yet. I have the same mindset when it comes to working out. While an intense body-building workout feels productive, that's not my focus in the gym.

With the goal of staying healthy and living longer, I strive to get my heart rate up for approximately twenty to thirty minutes a day. I may throw in some weights or core training after my cardio. This is enough to ensure I can keep up with my kids and ready myself for any family adventure, whether a hike or a bike ride. I plan to be right there with the rest of my family, or even ahead of them, so my daughters can see the importance of taking care of themselves.

In 2019, 20th Century Fox released a movie called *Breakthrough* in which a teenage boy falls through the ice and dies for a period of time. His mom, played by Chrissy Metz, cries and prays until all of a sudden, his pulse returns. In one scene, Chrissy's character's blood sugar spikes. Feeling dizzy, she needs to lay down in a separate hospital room. It really hit me when I realized that this mother's health caused her to struggle as she longed to stay by her son's side.

The source of Chrissy's character's health setback was never discussed in the movie, nor is it relevant. But in that moment, I committed that, as long as I have good health, I will make a conscious effort to invest in the parts that I can control – my diet and exercise. If any of my children need me by their side, I vowed I will always be able to keep up. I refuse to be the mom who can't be there because I stopped becoming my best self for them. Whether they need me for the memories we are creating or for their own health, I will make sure I have the energy and stamina for them.

Yet, as noble as this sounds, there are days I fight myself to keep that commitment.

ENERGY CREATES ENERGY

There are days I am just not feeling it. By it, I mean anything. I have no motivation to be productive, and even basic human functioning has left my radar. By five or six in the evening, the couch calls for me. I promise I'll sit just for a minute, but the minutes keep ticking until I no longer want to get up. I open my phone and start scrolling – someone got a puppy, another is proud of themselves for cleaning their house, and someone else posted a funny video I have to watch three times.

For years, there were very few evenings I could just sit after a long day. Clients called after hours, the kids needed a chauffeur, or errands stole my time.

Then, as if overnight, interest rates rose so work slowed, Alexis began driving herself, and Hannah reached an age where she spent more time with friends. Finley was still in the house, but there was less to keep me busy. I began using that extra time to rest. I felt I needed it after so many years of hustle. Then I rested more often, for longer and longer, until there were evenings I never moved from that couch.

Next, I stopped getting up as early and my journaling became the mindless blabbering of a toddler. My writing lacked substance. It was apparent I had lost any drive, motivation, or appreciation for what I had in my life. I was no longer living the way I wanted to teach my children to live, and I knew I wasn't showing up as my best self. Something had to change.

I realized I had connected my value to what I did, or how much I accomplished, and with work slowing down, I felt I had lost my value. It was time to reinvent myself, but before I could do that, I had to stop feeling sorry for myself.

Time is scarce and wasting it doesn't feel good. Rest is important, but this was no longer rest. This wasn't family time or hobby time. I just sat mindlessly. Though we can't be in 'go' mode all the time, I was choosing to read random Instagram posts over reading with Finley. Or opting for Netflix over sitting in Alexis' room and listening to the latest news in her life.

One day, I had enough. Absolutely enough. The laziness and lack of discipline flipped like a switch and turned to rage. I was angry about the days I had wasted and furious that I'd lost sight of who I was. I used this emotion to fuel me, and I immediately changed my clothes and hit the treadmill. It wasn't a fast workout. As a matter of fact, I only walked a mile or two to break a sweat, but for the first time in weeks, I felt…awake!

That's when I learned – *energy creates energy!* And this became my new mantra.

We all know the difference between rest and waste. Rest is amazing and we should practice it more often. Rest days may include doing nothing, reading a book, enjoying a walk, ignoring emails, or spending time with loved ones. It's up to you to decide how to use your rest time wisely, but you know what constitutes true rest, and if you listen to your body, you'll know when you need it, too. If you don't know what you are capable of, I am telling you now that you are capable of great things, so I hope that you, too, get angry when you find yourself wasting. You have too much to give.

Sitting just made me want to sit more, so I needed to eliminate that option. Moving my body not only made me want to move more, it also made me want to laugh and engage with others. I loved it. After my walk, I made sure to avoid the couch. Instead, I spent time with family or worked on an exciting project with renewed strength.

If you have a time each day when you begin to feel your energy drain, I encourage you to set a daily 'Energy Creates Energy' calendar alert on your phone at that anticipated time. When you see these words pop up on your screen, get up and move! If you are in an office setting, it may need to look more discreet, like walking to the bathroom or making fake copies, but simply rising from your desk can get your blood flowing. Any time you feel the wasted time calling you, no matter your surroundings, find a way to take action. Get your body moving and watch your mind follow.

YOUR VALUE

It took longer than it probably should have, but I eventually understood my value wasn't in my job. It wasn't in my title, and it wasn't in keeping up with the house. My value wasn't found in the things I did, but in how I did them. My value is in being a good mom and a good human, and in doing things the right way the first time because that's who I am.

My value was in living the way I wanted my children to live.

I needed that time on the couch in order to lose myself so that I could gain new lessons and light a massive fire inside of me. I only needed to get off the couch once to create more energy and take my life back. With that fresh energy, I jumped out of bed early the next morning excited to challenge myself in my journal. After that self-reflection, I spent a little time meditating – concentrating on my next chapter. Within a week, I was back on track, not only with my disciplines, but with rebuilding my best self.

I had to accept that a lighter workload didn't change who I was or what I wanted to accomplish. Instead, this was the perfect time to take advantage of all the things I had been putting off. So, I made a list – which included writing a book – and got started immediately.

Even though I have a new, refreshed purpose, there are still days the couch calls to me. I will still sit, but I try my best to ensure it is true rest and not wasted time. I also give myself grace if I do spend a little extra time learning who got a new puppy and who cleaned their house today.

GIVE YOURSELF GRACE

My friend texted me recently, extremely excited and motivated about an idea she had for a new business. She ran it by me and I couldn't hide my enthusiasm for her. It was right up her alley. The perfect job that she would be great at and could grow to any size that fit her life at the time. I could feel the adrenaline in each new text as her brain kept coming up with so many cool ideas.

The next day, her texts sounded completely different. I could feel the defeat as she second-guessed the entire idea and was back to being unsure of herself. We had a few more exchanges until she admitted the problem. Like many, she has days she just feels bland, and she assumed that meant her idea must have been a bad idea if she couldn't feel excited about it two days in a row.

"Nope! I'm not going to let you bail on it that quick," I told her. "It sounds like this is just a blah day for you. Just because you don't seem excited about anything doesn't mean that your idea is bad. It means that today is not the day you are going to make any progress, so maybe taking a nap or reading a book is more suited for you right now."

Giving yourself permission to have a lazy day without feeling guilty can prevent brilliant ideas from getting thrown in the trash. Need to turn that lazy day around? Go for a walk, a bike ride, or any sort of physical activity. Forcing a little energy will create more energy. If none of that jump starts your idea again, at least you got your blood flowing. You can try again tomorrow.

Physical activity is a wonderful, but often overlooked drug that can fight many conditions such as the ughs, blahs, slumps, and funks. If you feel any of these moods coming on, get up and do something. Anything. Even minimal physical activity can be done in most environments, so there's no excuse to avoid movement.

Our bodies need to be taken care of in order to last longer. Even if you are young and in good health during your hustling years, you will eventually get to the reflective years, and what you did – or didn't do – to take care of yourself will begin to show. When your effort declines, your body declines. There is no staying even. You may never have a six-pack or run a marathon, but consistent upkeep is a large contributor to feeling balanced.

6

AREA THREE:
PERSONAL CONNECTIONS

Webster's Dictionary offers no formal definition for the words personal and connection together. But an internet search returns a broad range of interpretations, many of which claim that a 'personal connection' involves something deeper than an acquaintance or a short interaction.

What if that's wrong? What if personal connection means finding a way to make any connection, no matter how brief, more personal?

I was originally going to call this chapter 'Relationships,' spotlighting only certain people in our lives. I considered focusing on the importance of building, nourishing, and strengthening your most cherished relationships so you can enter your reflective years with the best people in your life and minimal regrets. You know, stuff you've heard a million times.

But what if we are too narrow-minded about which relationships are important? What if by only nourishing and building a select few relationships, we've been neglecting others that come into our lives? As a result, we've been missing a big chunk of the human experience.

And so I realized that calling this chapter 'Relationships,' focusing only on close friends, family, partners, and children, wouldn't cover all that we need to live a fulfilling life. While we should prioritize certain people and work to build deep, meaningful relationships with them, what if we aimed to make all connections more personal?

THE BARISTA

Whether in the drive thru or store, when you get your morning coffee, do you look the barista in the eye? Do you smile? Or are you staring at your phone, looking around, or lost in thought about your upcoming day, speaking robotically as you order?

Either way, your greeting and body language are sending a message. That brief encounter either says, "I care that you are here" or "I'm too wrapped up in myself to notice you exist." You can tell me the barista doesn't care; after all, s/he likely won't remember you anyway. But, what if any time two humans interacted, it's always considered personal? What if we took every exchange as an opportunity to add value, even if only through our facial expression or body language? What if the goal was not to be remembered, but to leave a lasting impression of kindness and good energy on those around us?

It's true that most interactions are forgotten – but maybe it's because so few of us make the effort to connect. Back to the barista, what if more and more people looked her in the eye, asked her about her day, and started caring less about the coffee and more about the person making it? Eventually, the entire coffee experience would change, if only for seconds.

These warm encounters would continue throughout your day just because of a few extra smiles and kind words. You'd find workers enjoying their jobs and finding satisfaction in the most menial tasks, all because people acknowledge them and appreciate their efforts. It starts with a small, conscious effort by each one of us to create the atmosphere we want to experience.

INDIFFERENCE ISN'T KINDNESS

I was in Target a couple years ago with Finley, who was young enough to sit in the front of the cart. The place was packed in anticipation of the Fourth of July. I had purchased a basketball hoop way too large to carry, so the cashier called for assistance. As I stood in his line and waited, I asked him about his day, then we proceeded to make jokes and small talk. I was stunned when he told me I was only the fifth person to be nice to him that day.

I'm not sure if I was more shocked that so few people were nice to him or that he kept track, but I jokingly asked him if his shift had just started. Maybe I was only the fifth person in line.

"Nope," he answered. "My shift is almost over, and it's been a busy day. So few people are nice anymore, it's easy to keep track."

How's that for a bombshell? So few people in a checkout line were kind that the cashier could keep track of them on one hand. At first, I pictured a store full of disgruntled customers throwing their merchandise and swearing at the cashier. Then I realized that most people who weren't kind weren't necessarily mean either. They were simply indifferent. Distracted by their kids or looking at their phones, never smiling or acknowledging the human that was serving them.

The cashier and I didn't exchange names, but we did add a level of joy to each other's day, even if briefly. My choosing to spend those sixty seconds interacting, instead of distracted, made a difference for both of us. That day, he left work feeling seen, and I left feeling humbled.

Those baristas you think don't notice you – they do. They may have pushed you out of their minds the moment you left, but they did form an opinion about you in those few seconds. You may not care what it was, but at least ask yourself if that opinion lines up with your values and character. Short interactions can make a big difference if done right. They can bring spark joy and remove loneliness in a world full of people.

TYPES OF CONNECTIONS

There are three types of connections in our lives, and each provides the opportunity to make deeper, more personal impacts.

1. Brief Interactions

In addition to the baristas and cashiers mentioned above, these could include slightly longer interactions, like a server waiting your table, or even shorter ones, like someone holding the door for you. The interaction may be a simple thank you, but a thank you may come across as generic or uplifting depending on your body language.

I have found several ways to embarrass a teenage girl, but apparently the worst offense is making small talk or complimenting a stranger. When I'm in a drive-thru trying to make a joke with the cashier, I guarantee there is a teenager beside me whispering, *Mom, stop it. Stop it, please. This is embarrassing.* And true, sometimes the interaction is awkward. If the cashier can't hear me or doesn't understand my humor, the whole thirty seconds is a mess. But more often than not, the short, genuine attempt trumps indifference.

Once, in an amusement park restroom, I told a random stranger that I liked her shirt. Instantly, I felt Hannah's glare and nudges trying to stop me. The stranger looked stunned and told me how she loved her new shirt, but had lacked the confidence to wear it. After kicking herself for spending the money, she finally decided to put it on, but had felt insecure about it all day.

That stranger strutted out of that bathroom with new confidence and a reminder to own her style and embrace who she is. Hannah saw firsthand the impact of kind words, and when we walked outside, I heard the stranger sharing my compliment with all her friends: "That old lady liked my shirt!" Her description wasn't exactly what I wanted to hear, but I knew this old lady had made her day.

We may never see any of these people again, but every time we give someone a moment like this – a chance to see they're valued and cared about – we also reinforce that same belief about ourselves.

2. Regular Acquaintances

You see the same person every day at work. You know her name and you know she has dogs because of the pictures on her desk. You say *good morning* before you immediately ask if she was able to finish reviewing the file you needed. She hands you the file and you move on with your day. Ouch. So cold.

For months, I had similar interactions with a member of my team. When Ava joined us, I let her know how excited I was to have her and warned her that I tend to be straight forward. "You won't get any fluff with me," I said, almost proudly. I thought I had covered all the necessary bases for good teamwork.

After a couple of months, Ava's work was fantastic, but her tone grew passive-aggressive. I would ask her about the Smith file and she would respond with, "I don't know, I have thirty files ahead of it." Ava understood the urgency of the Smith file, and knowing she didn't have thirty other files, I didn't understand the harsh tone. After asking her what was going on, Ava unloaded about how hard she worked, yet how under-appreciated she felt for all her efforts. I assured her of the value she brought and reminded her that my brevity wasn't personal. She felt better and went back to dominating her workload.

Until the next month, when her condescending tone began all over.

We had another talk. Again, Ava felt her work had no impact, and again, I assured her she was the most important member of the team. "No one is better!" I reaffirmed.

The meltdowns came monthly and became an emotional drain, not just for me and Ava, but for the whole team. At the first sign of oncoming trouble, I would pull Ava aside to remind her of her value.

Finally, I went to our operations manager and expressed my exhaustion about Ava's neediness. It was eye-opening when he explained that, although I had warned Ava about my laser-focused work tone, her goals weren't the same as mine. I was driven by achievements; she was driven by feeling value and appreciation.

There was nothing wrong with either of our styles – as long as I made sure to meet her needs, too.

For that to happen, I had to soften my approach. No more *'Anything new on the Smith file?'* in the email subject line. I opted for *'Happy Friday! When you get a chance, do you mind updating me on the Smith file? I know you have a few ahead of it. Thanks for the help.'*

These few extra words changed everything. I began using the same approach company-wide, and the gains were fantastic! For Ava, the constant need for reassurance reduced drastically, and I started becoming someone people enjoyed working with. Even better, the few extra words didn't require crossing any boundaries into each other's personal life.

I don't believe I was ever mean to Ava, but I wasn't giving her the time and effort she deserved as a person. All it took was a few extra seconds a day to change our team culture.

While your rank or position within a company is irrelevant to how you treat others, it may still be one of influence – just by its title. Leadership is expected at certain levels, so some employees may value themselves based on your communication towards them. Understanding this power can ignite an army to come together for a common mission, or cause one to fall apart. It's important to use your influence to empower.

If you see yourself as the Ava in your day-to-day, you too have the ability to bring influence and leadership into people's lives, even when management isn't meeting your needs. Although I take full responsibility for my poor communication with Ava initially, I also recognize the ways she encouraged others, even when she felt unfulfilled. She would send an appreciative response to anyone who reached out to her and crack jokes to lighten the serious work culture I had created. She taught me how to see past my goals to the great people who were in my life helping me meet them.

Zig Ziglar says, "You can have everything in life you want, if you will just help other people get what they want."

If your work environment falls short in a certain area, ask yourself how you can bridge the gap. If you think there should be more community – start an accountability group. Everyone has something they want to get better at and can use the extra nudge. If you feel no one is appreciated for the work they do – be their biggest cheerleader instead of complaining about management with them. If there's no fun in the office, send a joke of the day to those who need a boost.

My favorite joke:

What's the difference between a crocodile and an alligator?

One will see you after a while and one will see you later!

Pause for laughter…

And remember to always be kind.

> *"Be kind, not because of who they are,*
> *But because of who you are."*

—Tim Sanders

Be patient, not because of who they are, but because of who you are.

Be honest. Be generous. Be forgiving… Be…

…any word describing your character and who you want to show up as – because of who *you* are. Each connection should be positive, not because of the other person's behavior, but because of yours.

There will be times when your kindness will be tested and you'll have to choose whether or not to address the tester. For me, choosing to address an injustice or let it slide depends on who's on the other side of that conversation.

ARGUING WITH A FOOL

"Moron," he called me. His words came like a slap in the face. We weren't even talking politics, but my comment about current business led him to believe I was claiming support for an administrative policy he disagreed with. Not even aware of the policy, I was just answering his question, "How's business going?"

Now, this was someone I worked with on a regular basis, so I knew it wasn't like I could just cut ties. I also knew that his childish comment was nothing personal. I had been watching him spout his unsolicited political views for years. Usually our conversations were enjoyable, but the more consumed he'd become by the state of the economy, the more difficult it was to keep our conversations light. I had to choose whether to engage or disconnect when politics rose to the surface.

I heard a Doris Smith quote that's stuck with me for years: "Arguing with a fool just proves there are two." While I'm not against political discussions, even with people I disagree with, I only choose to have these conversations with people I believe are capable of *having a conversation*. Not with those who become angry at different viewpoints or revert to name-calling.

When I decide whether I'm going to have a difficult conversation with someone who hurt me, or someone I disagree with, I first ask myself if they're a fool. Do I believe they're capable of listening to and comprehending a different perspective? If so, I attempt to approach that discussion as tactfully as possible. If I feel like I'll be engaging with a fool, I avoid being the second one in that conversation.

3. Close Relationships

As I enter my reflective years, I hope the efforts and goals I put in during my hustling years were enough to maintain strong, healthy relationships. I don't know what the future holds, but I've promised myself I'll continue to put in the work to be better for my family in the way they need me to be.

CHILDREN –

I was sure I was right. What they'd done was wrong, but when my heartrate fell back to normal, I was always the one who had to apologize. If I was being honest, it was becoming a real problem. My discipline style was making the discipline itself null and void.

I knew I had to stop yelling at my daughters. Even if I was right, the yelling escalated so quickly, I lost all credibility and the situation ended with me asking their forgiveness, instead of teaching any sort of valuable lesson.

After the ugly scene, I'd spend the next few hours battling guilt, vowing to never yell at my children again. Well, not at the decibels that required apology texts to the neighbors.

For days, and sometimes weeks, I kept my promise and communicated in an ordinary octave range. At least until I'd walk into a kitchen full of stuff. Stuff everywhere. One day, there were bookbags with their contents strewn across the floor. There was an arts and crafts explosion on the table that hadn't been touched for two days. There were eight blankets on the floor and a milk jug getting warm on the counter.

I'd take a few breaths, and remind myself that the mess meant there were little angels living in the home... but I still felt my face turn red and the vein on my forehead twitch. They *knew* better. I didn't require perfection, but at a minimum, perishable items should be put back in the fridge. If there was a normal-size, non-superhero mom version of the Hulk, that's what I'd begin to look like. I'd fight to contain my anger, but after looking around the room, I already knew in about thirty minutes I'd be the one apologizing.

It was an ugly cycle that forced Alexis and Hannah to read my face to determine my mood as I entered a room. They could feel my reaction coming to the surface before I could. It wasn't what I wanted.

What I did want was for my children to put their stuff away and make their own good choices. Not out of fear, but out of their ability to determine what's best for each situation and themselves. But I wasn't giving them the opportunity to exercise good judgment. I was on the attack before they could think through whatever action – or non-action – they were taking.

Over time, and with lots of practice, I was able to calm the vein in my forehead before it began to throb. If I sensed my body flipping to Hulk mode, I would immediately remove myself from the room, take as many deep breaths as needed, and try again.

~~BECAUSE I SAID SO~~ ACTIONS HAVE CONSEQUENCES

As the girls were getting older, I knew I needed them to begin trusting themselves to make the right decisions. Fear of mom was not the answer. But how could I teach my children to make the best decisions without always being there for each one they needed to make?

Then I watched a friend interact with her three adult children and realized they had built the relationship I was hoping to have one day. I asked her how she'd raised such empathetic kids filled with common sense, whom she maintained such great relationships with.

"I never told them no," she responded. Shocked, I immediately asked for more information. She went on to explain that it wasn't her job to shelter her children, but to guide them. Instead of telling them no, she would challenge them to weigh each decision's reward or consequence, and from a young age, they were given the skills to figure it out for themselves.

The motto in our home went from "Because I said so" to "Actions have consequences." It was difficult to relinquish my power; however, giving the girls authority to make their own decisions taught them important lessons. We're still there to guide them through each option, but when we empower them to make tough decisions, they treat themselves like adults and consider their future instead of our reactions.

SPOUSE/PARTNERS –

Early in our marriage, a friend invited Scott and I to a marriage retreat at his church. He assured us it was necessary to be around like-minded people engaging in the work required for a lasting marriage.

We signed up and spent the weekend with at least fifty other couples, attending several marriage building workshops with a guest speaker. There were many great take-aways, including couple goal-setting and distributing leadership roles within our family. But it was overshadowed by another theme – marriage is work. So much work that there should always be something to work on.

Many of the couples walked into the retreat excited to spend a weekend with each other, their friends, and no kids. Many of those same couples walked out angry and overwhelmed, carrying a laundry list of things they needed to do to grow as a couple.

The speaker challenged couples to identify pet peeves in their relationship and dig deep to find the underlying causes for these habits. For a visual, he brought a couple celebrating over twenty years together onto the stage, and what started as laughter quickly took a hard turn.

Speaker to the wife: "What's one thing that annoys you about your husband?"

Wife: "He leaves his clothes on the floor after work."

Speaker: "Why does that bother you?"

Wife: "I work hard to keep up with the house. It feels disrespectful."

Husband: "I work hard and just want to change my clothes and relax after work."

Speaker to wife: "Why?"

Speaker to husband: "Why?"

Speaker to wife: "Why?"

He continued the back and forth, pushing each spouse to find another reason this pet peeve was preventing them from true relational happiness, until one of them finally broke.

Wife: "It's because your mother spoiled you and now you act like I'm your mother! I can't be your wife until you start treating me like one!"

Total silence filled the room as the dust settled. We were stunned to hear that annoying habits are rooted in careless upbringings and need to be dissected to such a degree. Eventually, the speaker jumped back in with tips to rebuild this two-decades-old marriage that suddenly appeared in ruin.

The rest of the weekend went on like this and soon Scott and I found ourselves nitpicking at each other's flaws in the name of repairing damage we weren't even aware of. Luckily, after a couple of weeks of this nonsense, we finally stopped and asked each other, "Are these nuances really problems, or are we creating problems where there aren't any?"

While it infuriates me to find socks buried between couch cushions, I either remind Scott to grab his socks before he gets up, or I just pick them up myself and move on with my life. I did snap the day I found seven socks, and spiraled into an "I feel disrespected" tirade, but I picked up the socks and moved on. We didn't explore his childhood. Sometimes abandoned socks are just about the socks, nothing more.

In a relationship, some conversations can feel mundane, but it's better to prepare topics that excite you than to create problems for the thrill of the fight.

PREVENTATIVE CARE

As our nineteen-year anniversary quickly approaches, we continue to put in the work, not only to avoid creating fictional problems, but to prevent them. Some of that work includes:

• DATE NIGHTS – Whether the kids are young and dependent, older and indifferent, or there aren't kids at all, spending a little time focused on each other goes a long way. Hearing what's going on in each other's lives, reminiscing about fun times, or planning for the next memories are the incredible ways to reconnect. But date nights can also be a drag if not well prepared.

One date night, after days of chauffeuring kids to practice, attempting to assist with Common Core math, and getting sucked into the vortex of busy, our entire discussion consisted of how often we needed to replace our kitchen sponges. Not exactly a sexy conversation. I felt discouraged that valuable time together was wasted on kitchen accessories.

In order to be more prepared, we now pick topics, goals, or future plans to discuss in advance of our date night. Things that excite and keep us motivated during the days we hardly see each other while we divide and conquer our parenting duties.

- INTIMACY – An important part of any relationship, and possibly the most complex. I had a friend who told me she didn't like to have sex anymore. She assured me her spouse was fine with it. Perhaps so, and although I don't recommend creating problems where there are none, if you've removed intimacy and your partner just seems 'fine,' maybe it's time to work on your communication. Your spouse may have accepted your decision because of their commitment to the marriage, but does anyone want to go through life just 'fine'? Does a 'fine' relationship excite you? How long can 'fine' last? It'll take effort, and maybe even a counselor, but challenge yourselves to take your marriage from fine to fun.

- GRATEFULNESS JOURNAL – Nineteen years is a long time. A very long time. Some days I'm annoyed at the couch socks. Some days, I'm annoyed he's standing in front of every drawer in the kitchen that I need to get into. Some days, he's breathing too loud.

On these days, I recognize that I'm the problem and need a mindset shift. I know asking Scott to alter his breathing isn't the answer. For this, I turn to my journal to remind myself of the good qualities and shake out the gunk in my head until I'm ready to tackle the day. I move my focus to the big picture, eliminating problems that aren't really problems.

~ ~ ~

Building all connections is a vital aspect of the 4 Areas of Life. Each unique connection brings awareness and empathy, and helps build a world that's bigger than you, your family, and your friends. You'll receive as much new energy and support as you give, and you'll have stronger perceptions of people and deeper relationships as the years progress.

Bring joy – not because of who they are, but because of who you are. People are drawn to happy, passionate people, and happiness is just as infectious as misery. Even if you don't have the time to connect, share the energy you do have and take a second to see others.

I've spoken with many who've expressed feelings of loneliness at times, even when surrounded by others. We often pass people on the street, or sit in their vicinity and never acknowledge anyone is there. It's easy to feel lonely in a crowd if no one notices you exist. Be the one who sees others. A person can change a single experience, day, or life by making every connection personal. Let it be you.

7

AREA FOUR:
FINANCIAL

Early in our marriage, Scott and I got along great twenty-nine days out of the month. The thirtieth day was Discover Card's billing cycle. This was a long time ago, so it was actually the day the mailman would drop off the bill. I would grab it out of the mailbox, excited to see how much the balance had gone down after our last large payment, only to lose it when the balance was higher than the month before! I would unleash a torrent of curses and threats before I made it back into the house. Thankfully, this was also before video doorbells.

Are you kidding me!?

I would immediately call Scott to interrogate his every expense. I questioned his meal choices and accused him of springing for the unnecessary appetizer. We debated how often the oil really needed changed. I evolved into a monster as I read off each new credit card charge. We were young, we had two small kids, and we were broke. I was scared and using anger to persuade him to change – blind to its opposite effects.

Even in the middle of my rampage, deep down I knew my behavior wasn't going to solve anything. This before I implemented *The Disciplines* I promise to tell you about in the next chapter. My frustration, and lack of control over it, made me pretty unreasonable.

Financial insecurity can make you do and say crazy things. I was full of blame, but I haven't told you how many of those charges were mine. In my head, all of my expenses were justified. I only ate out the days I didn't like anything in the house, or if I craved Chipotle. I'd like to say that last sentence was sarcasm, but sadly, my cravings were costing us hundreds of dollars a month.

We had a problem. We may or may not have been at risk of losing our home, but the reality was, we were at risk of everything. We lacked direction and discipline, and had never identified our financial priorities. We wanted to have money in the bank, live comfortably, and retire well, but we never once talked about how we'd get there. Our Discover statement made it look like our goal was to spend the rest of our lives at every chain restaurant in the county. We lived under the assumption that if we just worked hard, everything would happen the way things are supposed to and the money would just be there.

And we did work hard. We hustled. Before I became a loan officer, I worked as a teacher during the day, a loan processor in the evening, and sold items on eBay at night. We kept our heads above water, but could never keep anything in the bank. Even worse, we began accumulating debt because we assumed we were making enough money to pay it off. I felt like a hamster spinning on a wheel. As the months went on, those happy twenty-nine days started getting cloudier. Financial frustration and insecurity snuck up on us, and one out-of-control credit card caused a crack in our entire foundation.

We needed to do something while it was manageable. Scott and I had similar financial upbringings. Neither of our parents used credit cards, as they all believed in being debt free. At one point in our early years, I called my parents to suggest they take advantage of the convenience of revolving debt. "You can still pay it off each month! Think of how many more things you could have!" I may have even implied how much smarter I was because of my platinum status. I was stupid.

FACE THE NUMBERS

First, we had to take a cold, painful look at what our income and expenses were. With all the hours we were putting in, we assumed we were doing well, but had no idea how much was actually coming in and how much was going out. When we added up how much we spent on eating out, we discovered it was approximately 25% of our income – unbelievable! The credit card statement was ruthless, revealing a variety of unnecessary charges. My stomach hurt just looking at it.

Scott and I knew we had to figure this out together, without blame, which made it that much harder. Blame can create a defensiveness that prevents you from being open-minded. Being open-minded is a requirement to get back on the right track. For us, there was nothing to blame; just something to fix.

Before you can figure out how you are going to get to your financial destination, you have to decide where that destination is. You've already been driving aimlessly; it's time to define your financial values and goals. Really dig in to better understand what makes you feel secure and get to the reflective stage with few regrets. A few examples:

- I want to be debt free except for the house in X years.
- I want to use cash for all expenses except X (if any).
- I will only use debt for X so that I can use the cash for other investments.
- We are going to live on one income beginning X.
- We are only going to live on X percent of our income.
- I will pay myself X amount or percent each pay.
- I want to have X in savings by X year.
- I will buy a car based on the purchase price, not the payment.

You may have noticed a couple of these examples contradict each other. This list needs to be about *your* values and what *you* want for yourself financially. My intention was to show you different perspectives.

You can tweak your list as you reassess your goals, but never compromise the things you want most for what's easiest now. The point is to clearly define what you will and won't allow your money to do, then live by those values.

If you are completing this activity as a couple, you may find you have competing values. Do not give up hope! Combining two different money mindsets may be an obstacle, but there is nothing wrong with a good challenge. One person may bring a little fun to the mix, while the other keeps things on track. Just remember to reward yourselves for each milestone. As you could tell by our spending, I loved going out to eat, so when we hit certain goals, we'd celebrate our victory with a night out.

With our commitment to get out of debt and our continued dedication to hustle, we became debt free and living by our clearly defined values within two years. We started getting along all thirty days of the month and knew our financial goals were being met. How were we sure? Simple – we had written them down and measured our progress so our destination was clear.

KNOW WHERE IT GOES

Many live under the misconception that proper money management and budgeting are only for those within a certain income range. They assume no one who makes six figures should be on a budget. Why would they need to? Sadly, I've encountered several families who make $100,000-250,000 annually and have no idea where their money goes each month. And the more they make, the faster it disappears.

Here's a real-life example: I met with a couple who had two $800 car payments a month. So, we start with $1600 and add in their $3000 house payment, and $50 in minimum credit card payments. Since they pay their entire card balances off monthly, $2500 is a more accurate figure. Throw in the $200 minimum payment on a couple of old student loans and our total comes to $7300 in expenses a month. Assuming utilities, gas, and groceries are already included in the credit card balance, we will leave those necessities out.

This couple grossed $125,000 annually, or $10,416 a month. With a 30% withholding for taxes, that is now $7,291 for their monthly take-home pay. They are spending every dollar that they are earning.

I have seen this scenario time and time again. The couple is making "good" money, has low interest rates on all their debts, and nothing appears broken. Life gets busy and since everything seems to be going as planned, there's no need to give it another thought. They likely won't stop to ask where their money went until their reflective years. By then, it will be too late.

RELATIONSHIPS WITH MONEY

I had no idea finding the right relationship with money was like dating. Money is money, right? But if that's the case, why do we act funny around it? Why do we chase it? Why are we mad when it's not there for us, and why can it lead us to so much regret? Have you ever woken up feeling remorseful about what you did with money the day before? Your relationship with money will be the longest relationship you'll ever have. It may take years of effort, and possibly therapy, before you have a healthy relationship with money.

Like everything else in life, we learn about money from the people who raised us. Maybe that there was never enough or it always disappeared without knowing where it went. Perhaps your family lived comfortably, but you never saw how much work it took behind the scenes, leaving you to assume money will always be there.

When I grew up to realize my own relationship with money was messy, I spent a lot of time not only redefining it, but also trying to understand where these beliefs came from. In our youth, my brother and I always had food on the table and were loved; however, we didn't have much else. Cable TV was a luxury, and there was no way my parents would spring for the caller ID on our landline, forcing us to answer calls without knowing who it was. We also couldn't afford new cars – or used ones. As a matter of fact, most of the vehicles we had during my high school years were given to us from members of our church. The cars were old and had too many issues to justify trading them in, so the owners felt passing them down to us was a good way to be charitable – they were right.

In college, I had friends who clearly didn't share the same struggles. Once, a roommate dumped all her change on the ground in a drive-thru because "it made her purse heavy." I was shocked. She threw away actual money because of its inconvenience. I went back to that Taco Bell later in the day to pick up what I could. In spite of the fact that she appeared too nonchalant with money, she turned out to be a hard worker who earns her keep, but her lack of struggle gave her a completely different relationship with money than I had.

Although I recognize the character that hardships can create, I knew I didn't want my children to encounter the same struggles. The dilemma was ensuring they'd still acquire integrity and a strong work ethic without the same lessons growing up. We've decided the best way to do this is to open up all financial discussions to our children. We share our sources of income, the risks, the rewards, and what goes into our decision-making. We teach them it's more about the mindset than the numbers.

Alexis now has her first job and is understanding the value of work. She manages her own bank account and appreciates how many hours she'll need to work for a tank of gas. We do our best to guide her as she explores her own relationship with money.

FINANCIAL GUILT

A couple of years before Finley was born, I was feeling pretty motivated. I met with my boss and told him my goals, all of which would make it possible to pay off my mortgage. He looked at what I owed and helped me break down what I needed to accomplish each month, week, and day. We factored in taxes, living expenses, and potential unknowns. By the end of the conversation, I knew the exact number of phone calls I needed to make each hour to make this a reality.

That year, I exceeded my goals. I had set out to get a few years' worth of work done in one so I could further our family's path, and I had accomplished just that. The problem? I didn't think I could do it again. When my boss asked about my goals for the following year, I had nothing. He kept pushing, but I kept dodging any goal-related conversations. While he was questioning how much bigger I wanted to go, I began questioning if I even wanted to do this job anymore. Was I burned out? Was I afraid I would fail after setting the bar so high?

No, none of that. I felt guilty. I had made enough money to pay off all of our debt and put a little extra in the bank. I didn't think I deserved to make any more. I felt like I had taken a large chunk of my share all at once.

During my youth, when I spent a lot of time at the church, I remember the whispering between adults when a member of the congregation bought a brand-new car instead of used. There were a lot of opinions about the member's excess money and what it should have been used for instead.

"I can't believe he bought a brand-new car."

"I know. How selfish. Think of all the families he could have helped instead."

"The Bible says to be a good steward of your money."

"Christians should always buy used."

I heard Bible verses raining down to support their belief that this was not good, Christian behavior – possibly even a sin? My parents didn't feel this way, but they shared the different perspectives being argued by the others. I just wasn't mature enough to comprehend it all. I debated in my own head what I thought of buying a new car – and I didn't even drive yet. I never reached a resolution about it being right or wrong. I was just relieved that it would be years before I would have to.

Twenty years later, when faced with buying a new or used truck, I felt the guilt I'd been introduced to years ago start to rise up inside of me. The same debate began in my head. Would buying new take away from others I could help? Was I being financially responsible?

With my boss also pushing for my goals, it was time to sit down and confront what was holding me back. I started to unfold my complicated feelings associated with money and sort out truth from fiction. I worked for what I had, yet felt like a fraud. I kept feeling it was time to go back to earning what I truly deserved – not much.

Then, three years later, I came across a book by Dan Sullivan called *Wanting What You Want*. What a game changer! It's small, but packed with information. The moment of change came in the line:

"...the single most important thing to understand about this 'wanting' skill is that the reason you want something is because you want it. Period."

Poof. That was it. I didn't have to limit myself to the things I needed. I had permission to want things also. I could want them just because I wanted them – with no justification.

Guess who bought a brand-new truck! Why? Because I wanted to. I'm not talking about a child throwing an "I want it" temper tantrum. I did my research, shopped around, and found the vehicle that held the best value, as well as all the car seats. Once I confirmed this vehicle fit our current and long-term financial plan, I owned my decision and moved on.

CHOOSE ABUNDANCE

Dan's book also introduced me to the terms scarcity and abundance. I had spent my entire life viewing money as scarce, believing there was only so much to go around. Anything extra was taking from others. I had never considered the possibility of money as abundant. This new viewpoint allowed me to break free of my never-enough mentality. I was given permission to accept anything I worked for. I can have mine, and you can have yours too! We aren't competing for the same prize; we can all do excellent work and reap the benefits. There is no guilt in that!

I learned to rebuild my relationship with money, and you can too. The hardest part is identifying the myths that hold you back. For me, a small book made everything click. The best way to understand your relationship is to start asking simple questions:

- What did you grow up hearing about money?
- How did that impact you?
- Is money good? Is money bad?
- Does what you have today bring guilt, frustration, or happiness?
- Do you chase money? Is it elusive?
- Is there enough to go around or are you competing?
- How do you feel when someone else gets what you want?
- How do you *think* you should feel about money?
- What mindset changes would it take to feel that way today?

It's easy to assume you'll be secure and content when you feel you have 'enough,' but more money can easily lead to more wanting. A healthy relationship is one that includes gratitude even when it falls short of your expectations. Ultimately, what happens in your finances is your responsibility, no matter what wrenches were tossed in your plan. So, if you aren't at peace with your finances today, change must start with you.

We also have a duty to have the right conversations with our children. I was tested the day Finley wanted to buy a cheap toy. I really didn't want any more junk toys collecting in the living room, but I told her we didn't have enough money. She asked how much we had and offered to empty her piggy bank to put it towards the purchase. I had to consider my next move and finally settled on explaining that we did have enough money to buy the toy, but I knew she wouldn't play with it for long, and we didn't want to waste the money we had worked so hard for. We talked about what she did with her toys, the difference between wants and needs, and how we make decisions on what we should buy. The answers we give children today could define their relationship with money tomorrow.

This conversation led me to ask myself – what is enough?

WHAT IS ENOUGH?

Webster's Dictionary defines enough as an adjective: "occurring in such quantity, quality, or scope as to fully meet demands, needs, or expectations."

What does enough mean to you? If your initial demands, needs, or expectations are met, will you be at peace? Have you ever considered what your demands and needs are?

Enough is so much more than a number – it's a state of mind. And don't confuse enough with settling. I hope you stay hungry and accomplish everything you want, long after you reach enough.

Enough is when you no longer need or want – but you can still chase! You can still challenge yourself, take risks, and continue to build a legacy. But the decision to do so is driven by passion, not fear. Enough comes with contentment, not dollar signs.

The real estate industry can be temperamental, leaving those involved with a mix of financial highs and daunting lows in their career. To prepare, many save as much as possible to ensure their security during the lows. Then, they panic at the first touch of their savings. Fear rushes in, frantic choices get made, and enough fades away.

These fears come from a scarcity mindset. This mindset forgets that if money runs out, more can be earned. It doesn't see the multitude of opportunities available to us no matter the economy. And the scarcity mindset refuses to acknowledge that even in worse-case scenarios, humans can be resilient and find ways to navigate through.

Many of these fears connect back to your beliefs about money and require you to retrain your brain.

I have friends living paycheck to paycheck. They reside in a constant state of worry. No matter what they have, it will never be enough. They buy a brand-new vehicle each time one needs replaced (it's not a sin, I know!), then worry about making the payment each month – yet justify new as their only option. Their quarterly bonuses will relieve some of the burden, but before those checks clear, they go back to worrying about the next month.

Over the years, we've had several money conversations with these friends. I try to give some guidance, but am blocked with the reasons why budgeting won't work and they just can't get ahead. Our conversations have shown me that they have never appreciated what they have. They have always made their payments, but have never been thankful when the last bill was paid, always opting for immediate worry at the next month's bills set to flood in. Worry and fear have actually become comfortable emotions for them. Even in the good times, they are waiting for the bad.

Do you know these types of people? Are you these people? Do you ever stop long enough to give thanks or just appreciate how good it feels to make ends meet in a time when you are consumed with worry? Little moments of gratitude will show us the opposite side of worry and even break up the muscle memory of fear. When you live in fear all the time, you instinctively turn to fear as your most common reaction. Adding in some gratitude will give you a second reaction to choose from. Practice will eventually make gratitude your new go-to emotion.

Do you know what else happens when you start choosing gratitude? Since appreciation breeds appreciation, you'll start to feel your new abundant mindset taking over. You'll find you have enough sooner than expected, and feel confident there is plenty more to come. Your openness will allow more to get in. Living in fear and worry closes the door to keep anything from escaping, which also blocks new gifts from coming in.

Strive for enough, but live with contentment and gratitude. Giving thanks for what's in front of you is the quickest way to ensure you don't get lost in the pursuit of the things you are chasing.

Be thankful for all you have, all you have lost, and for the abundance in this world that is yet to be yours.

8

THE DISCIPLINES

It's early, I'm the only one awake, and I'm staring at a blank page in my journal. I bought a Five Star college-ruled notebook with the binders and Post-It notes and apparently, it's just as expensive as a fancy new journal that says something inspirational like 'I Believe' on the cover. I like my notebook better.

I'm not sure what to write about yet. Experts recommend listing things you are thankful for. Articles I've read suggest writing about self-reflection or setting goals you'd like to accomplish. All I know is the way I feel leaves me with little options. Am I anxious, overwhelmed, angry, etc.? Trying to figure that out seems like a good start.

I look around the house at the mess. If I do have time to clean, everyone's stuff reappears and I feel like I can't keep up. Though my two young children are usually well behaved, they will scream incessantly when I'm on the phone. There's always piles of paperwork to do, and I worry Scott and I have nothing to talk about except the kids. These are issues that haunt many young parents, but I refuse to settle for "that's just the way it is." It's messy in my head, and I realize that's when I have to make a change. What's in my mind has to be clear to help me get a grasp of the rest.

It's been eight years since I picked out that Five Star notebook, and it has changed my life. I've written thousands of words, from brilliant ideas to mindless drivel. I've made creative lists that don't relate to anything in my life, but help keep my brain active. I've used this journal numerous mornings to give myself a pep talk that took me from flopping out of bed to feeling unstoppable.

When the journaling started, I used it to identify and control the chaos in my head. Sometimes that meant a lot of writing about nothing – just writing until my mind was rested enough to engage with others. From there, it evolved. Through the calming effect of writing, I found my mind lied to me – a lot.

I often asked myself why I felt the way I did under certain circumstances. For instance, why did I feel like a failure when I couldn't keep up with basic household chores? The cleanliness of the house shouldn't define me, yet it was a huge source of discomfort. The myth in my head told me a clean house was a sign of having your life under control.

The truth was that I grew up in a spotless home with a mother who didn't work outside the house. We had rooms she wouldn't let us enter in order to keep them spotless. They ended up dank and musty because there was no life running through them, but I guess it didn't matter because no one was allowed in anyways.

I had been lying to myself for years about what a clean house meant to me – and about me – and it wasn't until I sorted through it in my journal that I finally saw the truth. My value didn't come from never having dirty dishes in the sink. My value didn't come from clean floors or folded clothes. Through writing, I found my value was giving them a safe, comfortable place to call home, not how stuff was organized.

As my journaling evolved, I began challenging myself with tough questions that I forced myself to answer honestly. Questions like:

- What does my future self look like? What is one action I need to take today to get there?
- At the end of my days, if someone asked what I regretted most in my life, what would my answer be?
- In regards to a recent situation in life or work that required my involvement – how would my future self handle this differently than the person I am today?
- If I had to write my own eulogy, what would it say? (Morbid to some, yet this had an exceptional impact in my life. I unexpectedly filled pages with all the things I didn't do because of my excuses or fears. It created a fire in me to accomplish those things while I can.)

As a result of this reflection, I started becoming my future self and handling situations as the person I wanted to be, not the person I was. I kept upping my game and continued defining a better self so each version of the person I was becoming was better than the last.

LOVE YOURSELF FIRST

Recently, I told my husband about a difficult co-worker and explained how she's great at her job, but exhausting. She's often emotional, snaps at others, and will break down unexpectedly when she becomes stressed. Every time I saw her name pop up on my phone, I felt a twist in the pit of my stomach because her mood was unpredictable. I never knew if she was going to be kind or threatening.

Scott made a good point: "That sounds like you eight years ago." Ouch! But he was right. When I became stressed or overwhelmed, others weren't sure if Fun Jessie or Angry Jessie would send the next email. I asked him what he thought changed in my life, and he was quick to respond, "I think it was your journaling. You became a lot more stable when you started writing."

From there, I've added other activities to identify and maintain control of my emotions and get excited about my life.

I don't do these things because I know I will love my future self. I do them because I love myself already and want to be better.

I'm going to say that again to make sure it sticks – I don't practice these disciplines or take care of myself in order to be worthy enough to love myself someday. I do them today, because I love myself already, and I like to take care of the things I love.

This realization led me to what I call *The Disciplines*. These are small, vital tasks I complete in my life because I love myself and believe they will lead me to be in better shape mentally and physically.

At least five days a week, I incorporate five disciplines, many part of my morning routine:

1. Wake up early – 5 a.m. school days/6 a.m. no school
2. Journal
3. Meditate at least ten minutes
4. Consume less than twenty grams of sugar a day
5. Exercise at least thirty minutes

I created a monthly calendar in the back of my Five Star notebook that looks like this in order to track my disciplines:

Sunday	Monday	Tuesday	Wednesday	Thursday	Friday	Saturday
	1 5am Journal Exercise Sugar <20g Meditate	2 5am Exercise Sugar <20g	3 5am Journal Exercise Sugar <20g Meditate	4 5am Journal Sugar <20g Meditate	5 5am Journal Exercise Sugar <20g Meditate	6 Journal Exercise
7 Journal Sugar <20g Meditate	8 5am Journal Exercise Sugar <20g	9 5am Journal Exercise Sugar<20g Meditate	10 5am Exercise Sugar <20g Meditate	11 Journal Sugar <20g Meditate	12 5am Journal Exercise Sugar <20g Meditate	13 5am Journal
14	15 5am Journal Exercise Sugar <20g Meditate	16 5am Journal Sugar <20g Meditate	17 5am Journal Exercise Sugar <20g Meditate	18 5am Journal Exercise Sugar <20g Meditate	19 5am Journal Exercise Meditate	20 Exercise
21 5am Journal Sugar <20g	22 5am Journal Exercise Sugar <20g Meditate	23 5am Journal Exercise Sugar <20g Meditate	24 Exercise Sugar <20g Meditate	25 5am Journal Sugar <20g Meditate	26 5am Journal Exercise Sugar <20g Meditate	27 Journal Exercise Sugar <20g
28 Exercise Sugar <20g	29 5am Journal Exercise Sugar <20g Meditate	30 5am Journal Exercise Sugar <20g	31 5am Journal Exercise Sugar <20g Meditate			

There are many ways to create a tracking document on paper or digitally. Since it is part of my journal, it's easy to update daily before I begin my routine. Find the way that's best for you.

THE DISCIPLINES

Waking Up Early –

It wasn't easy getting started, and although it gets better as it goes, many mornings are as much of a struggle as in the beginning. I try to stay focused on how good I feel after. My wake-up time is five a.m. on school days and six a.m. on the others. I tried five a.m. daily, but found it better to use the extra hour as a reward if I've been hitting my morning goals.

Making the adjustment to getting up early can be an endeavor, but being tired the first couple of days helps. Avoid naps. After a day or two, you'll become tired enough to go to bed early, which makes it easier to get up early the next morning. It doesn't take long before your body adjusts. You may not need to get up as early depending on your morning responsibilities, but I challenge you to start with thirty minutes earlier for one month and reassess after that. Do you still feel rushed in the morning? Are there other activities you want to add into your schedule? Then work your way up earlier and earlier. Start with ten-minute increments until you feel like you have a good flow and can start your day satisfied, calm, and ready to conquer the world.

Trying to decide what you want to do in the morning? Ask yourself what needs to be done each day for you to start your day empowered and grow your future self. Get those things done and out of the way in the morning. Too much can come up during the day that prevents you from getting in your physical activity or any of your other disciplines.

Yes, I know some of you are great at committing to your disciplines at other times of the day. Maybe you meditate daily – at lunch. Or perhaps you haven't missed a scheduled workout in a year – after work. That's fantastic. You can still include a brief morning routine, because if you don't have one, I guarantee you'll find at least a few things you can do to get your mind in top shape for the day. An extra thirty minutes reading or stretching your body can go a long way before you have to engage with others. You may still need to decompress after a long day, but find morning activities that can help you get ready before the stress comes.

One of my favorite things about the early morning is that it's my time. I don't have to explain myself to anyone because no one needs help with homework while I'm reading a book. No one asks me where their folder is. The biggest obstacles to self-care are the responsibilities we have to other people. This allows time for myself – guilt free – to put myself first.

Some days I spend half my morning trying to convince myself that I'm not tired while fighting to keep my eyes open. Other mornings really flow. Don't worry if your mornings don't feel natural right away. You can tweak the order of your disciplines and continue to add and remove from your routine. Many choose not to do anything each day, so even small actions daily put you in an elite group.

Journaling –

I've touched on journaling already, but this can clearly be credited for one of my first transformations. I've already shared many ideas, and there are plenty of web sites that provide journaling topics if you become stuck. When all else fails, there are two go-to topics you can pull from any time:

1. Things to be grateful for
2. Set daily intentions

The first one is pretty self-explanatory. You can choose to list several items, or you can focus on one by soaking yourself in as much detail as possible. Describe the color, the feeling, and what value it adds to your life. Yes, you are thankful for your family, but why? What significance do they truly add? What are you learning from them? How can you strengthen your relationship and the character you want to instill in them?

The second item, setting daily intentions, gets overlooked a lot, yet can set your tone for the entire day. Even if it wears off after lunch, with practice you'll learn to make it last.

I spend fifteen to twenty minutes setting my intention for the day. I decide what characteristic I want to focus on growing, such as appreciation or patience. The more I immerse myself in what the intention should look like, the longer the feeling will linger.

One excerpt from my journal reads like this:

May 24th

Today I'm going to focus on being calm. As soon as I log in this morning, I know there will be numerous emails, and I will be tested. One of my clients is frustrated, and I need to call him instead of email. He is likely going to come at me hard, so it will be the perfect time to exercise calm today. If the interest rates drop again, it will lead to even more activity, but instead of feeling overwhelmed, I am going to approach each task like a cool breeze. If I'm clear and thorough in all my communication, I won't have to repeat any of my work and it will prevent situations from escalating. This little extra time up front will save me a lot of time later. I won't get frustrated, even when an unexpected fire pops up.

I won't get worked up if an appraisal comes in low. I know how to handle these situations in a professional manner. What if a client wants to cancel? Been there, too. I will try to work through their obstacles. If they still cancel, I'll replace them with two new clients. No matter what bounces all around me, I will remain calm throughout the day. I will take deep breaths and remind myself who I am and what I'm capable of.

You may find sticky notes on my computer that read "calm," "breathe" and "I can handle more than most." Use any resources available as a constant reminder to help you keep your commitments. I have a daily alert that pops up on my phone at three p.m. with the quote, "Teach the world how to treat Jessie." It's my constant reminder that my daily intention may be wearing off and the way I treat myself, as well as how I talk to myself, is how I teach others what I'm willing to tolerate in my life.

Meditating –

Nothing feels better than knowing you are in alignment with your purpose and making choices from the best version of yourself. You begin to find happiness not just in the victories, but also in the challenges. Your work brings you fulfillment as well. Many people know when they are in alignment, even if they call it something different like peace, contentment, or balance. It doesn't mean you've settled and stop growing; it simply means you've accepted yourself and your ability to listen. You've accepted where you are today and know that growth will continue if you patiently keep up with the work.

WHATEVER WORKS FOR YOU

Sit up straight, hands on knees, and no noise whatsoever. Keep your mind absolutely blank and push out any thoughts that sneak in. I thought that was the one and only way to meditate, but this didn't work for me. I hated it. It was too boring, too quiet, and too, well, awful. I sat in silence with no music or guidance fighting my attempt to keep thoughts out with thoughts about keeping thoughts out. It was as frustrating as that sounded. If I did stay awake, my back hurt from the stiff posture, and my hands got cold easily.

I decided meditation must require a person with a high level of emotional intelligence to be able to sit silently and clear their mind. I wasn't there yet so I stuck to journaling and figured one day I would try it again when I was ready to achieve a whole other level of greatness. This was beyond my skill level.

Then one day I was in a Zoom meeting with some other people in my industry during the COVID-19 shutdown. We were meeting monthly to share our experiences in such a crazy time, to offer support, tips, and feedback on how to keep moving forward in this new way of life. The topic of meditation came up and I was dumbfounded by what I heard. Some lie down to meditate. Some use meditation apps on their phones. There was no right or wrong way as long as you did something.

BETTER THAN PROS AND CONS

Now, after I spend a little time in my journal, I lay back in my chair, search 'meditation piano music' and close my eyes. If my room is in the 60-degree range, I'm under a blanket keeping my hands warm. If it's nice and warm, I might lay them face up to allow for maximum openness. Either way, I get comfortable. I let the thoughts come. Sometimes I start the meditation with no intentions and other times I lie back with a certain focus in mind.

For example, I was deciding between two job offers recently. On paper, offer A was a no-brainer. The stability, the business structure, and the potential were unmatched. Yet, I couldn't ignore the panic in my gut every time I tried signing the employment agreement. I took it to meditation and envisioned myself at each job the first week. Offer A was full of regret, frustration, and feeling trapped. Despite not seriously entertaining it initially, offer B felt full of peace, happiness, and even success.

Meditation showed the correct path. Offer A looked better to everyone else in the industry, but something bigger than me knew there were superior plans and I needed to accept offer B to stay on the right path.

These meditation practices are also how I committed to this book. Despite having the idea for eight years, it wasn't until I started meditating that I saw the entire book unfold in front of me. Every time I closed my eyes, I saw opportunity. I also saw the obstacles. When fear of criticism would overcome me, meditation showed me the gain was greater than the adversity, and that excitement inspired me to write a book in thirty-three days. That is the power of listening.

Not only does meditation lay out exciting paths and guide me through tough decisions, it also prepares me for battles. Literal battles. If I enter a room where my kids are fighting, I am much better equipped to handle it. I don't join the fight and yell at them for yelling. Instead, I'm able to diffuse the situation gently.

I don't meditate for long, and I may not be doing it "right", but I do it. What could you accomplish if you added meditation, or a similar exercise that you aren't doing now?

Reduce Your Sugar Intake –

It's been more than three years since my first experiment eliminating sugar, but this one simple change in my eating has impacted my life significantly. Since I already shared some of the major impacts in Chapter Five, I want to challenge you in this section.

Just reducing one ingredient gives me more energy during the day. The two-p.m. sluggishness? Gone! I can work all day without that mid-afternoon craving for a nap. I no longer have lows because

I'm no longer coming off artificial highs. My dentist even noticed a difference.

What small item can you reduce or eliminate in your diet that could have a significant, lasting impact?

At the beginning of the chapter, I told you I set these disciplines for only five days a week. We travel a lot for sports and like to go out on date nights. Staying up late and laughing over cocktails and desserts fulfills my personal connections, so it was important to reach an attainable goal with no guilt. Many weeks I achieve seven days with limited sugar. Some weeks I fall short. A discipline should be sustainable, not a short-term fix.

Whether you are bored, stressed, or just need a pick-me-up, you may face times in your day when you will have to choose between a Snickers or a water. Do you mindlessly grab the Snickers without considering water as an option? It may take a conscience effort to choose which will allow you to maintain your stamina and avoid unnecessary struggles. Putting these disciplines in place will optimize your mental strength, but until you get there, you may need an accountability partner. Find someone who will stop you before you can even get to the snacks. Better yet, if you can win the battles in the grocery store, the pantry is much easier to conquer.

Exercise —

For years, I heard people say that everything will start aching the day you turn forty. Well, I thought I could outsmart the naysayers by using mind over matter — then I turned forty. Suddenly, I heard all kinds of cracking noise when I stood up. It was my joints. ALL OF

THEM. There were random aches and pains in places that I didn't know existed. I couldn't sit or stand without sighing. It's impossible – like licking your elbow (did you just try it?). The more I worked out, the more my hips would ache. I would take rest days only to find out the lack of activity made my knees ache instead.

Pain seemed to be unavoidable. I could either take care of my body and be sore or let it go and be sore. I decided to keep icing the hips and stick to the healthier way to be sore. At least this way, I'd gain flexibility and energy in my soreness – as well as confidence in myself each time I pushed through.

I didn't start exercising until I had children. In my twenties, exercise was all about controlling weight. I chased a number on a scale. Sadly, that number gave me confidence or destroyed it. And since I had no other purpose for working out, I'd hit my goal, stop exercising, gain the weight back, and start exercising again. Rinse and repeat.

Then a good friend let me know about her impending divorce after ten years of marriage. Eager to get her finances and health in order, she shared her excitement for the new life she was creating. She confessed, "I am losing weight so I can look hot for the next one." I laughed, uncomfortably, as the comment lingered in my head. What if she had put that effort into herself during her marriage, not for her spouse, but for herself?

Why do we let ourselves go for the one we love, but construct a better self for strangers? It's not the weight I'm referring to. The responsibility we take for our own happiness is what is attractive to others, and also fills a void that we often expect our partners to fill.

The confidence and independence my friend began building in herself would have been invaluable to her marriage.

Many times, I have put the responsibility for my happiness in Scott's lap. That was unfair to him, and left me powerless over my life. In my friend's situation, she blamed her husband for her emptiness, and was looking for the next partner to fill that gap. Ironically, she was filling it herself by doing the things she didn't do while she was married. She may find another partner who makes her happy, but if she stops taking care of her mind, body, and finances – will he be enough?

Attraction to each other is far greater than the physical. Happiness, confidence, independence, and self-love are all vibes that radiates off of us. Are we sharing our best self with our partner? Or are we constantly sharing our worst and wondering why they don't make us happy?

A lot of this happiness and confidence comes from our physical health. We gain assurance from promises we keep to ourselves to look and feel a certain way. We enter a situation with the right mindset, instead of hoping our partner will fix our mood.

After the conversation with my friend, I realized I didn't want it to be Scott's responsibility to inspire me to better. I was going to inspire myself, and share my best with the people already in my life.

DO IT FOR THOSE WATCHING

Imagine your children are more of what you are. If you are unhealthy, they are likely to pick up the same habits, even earlier. If you are constantly overreacting and unaware of how your moods affect others, they are likely to have even less emotional awareness. Their only hope will be breaking the cycle.

Since they are watching you, you are giving your children a running start with your habits and behaviors. Will they eat even more processed foods and sweets, or will they be disciplined when it comes to mindless eating? Will they blame everyone for everything wrong in their lives, or will they take responsibility to create the best life possible? Will they challenge themselves and try new things, or will they play it safe? *Live the life you want to teach your children to live.*

Before you feel overwhelmed about how much you need to do to grow, you should know, I did not start with all five disciplines at once. It began with getting up early just to bring peace to my family and our morning routine. Then it evolved as I mixed in some journaling. I threw in the other disciplines one by one as I was ready for more growth in my life.

I continue to add and adjust as I constantly define my future self and determine which skills I need to develop further. You may find your disciplines vary greatly from mine. It's your life. Make it what's best for you.

PART THREE

Betting on Yourself

9

LOVE YOURSELF DESPITE, NOT BECAUSE

In order to achieve peace and happiness, we have to start with loving ourselves. Unfortunately, too many people have a list of things they want to change before they can see their worth. They tend to see value in their future self, when they behave a certain way or reach certain accomplishments, but not as they are right now. Yet once they become their better self, they still see themselves as flawed, still unable to be loved.

Loving yourself begins by retraining your brain. We've been programmed to ask ourselves why we love something. We judge how something looks and feels to determine our feelings toward it. We end up applying the same principle to ourselves, and when we don't have a strong enough reason, we assume we aren't worthy of self-love. I want to challenge you to rethink your motivation for loving yourself.

When you learn to love yourself despite what you believe makes you unworthy, not because of all the things that make you desirable, you will want to do more for yourself.

START WITH YOUR BODY

I still haven't hit my weight and strength goals, but I love my body despite this. And I'm not waiting until I hit those goals to love it. Because I love it as it is, I choose to take care of it. I want to make sure my choices work toward being fit and healthy to maintain a high level of energy to be ready for anything.

If you don't fully accept and love your body until, or unless, it looks a certain way, that day may never come. However, if you love it despite your shortcomings, you'll get to look back at your body and know you were kind to it. Love it as is. Right now. Love it despite the way it has been abused – by you or by others.

Loving your body is a choice every day. Each time you look in the mirror, or feel the curves going in the wrong direction, you choose whether to embrace it or reject it. Don't blame your body for your choices, either. Your body keeps you going even when you don't give it the right fuel.

LOVE IT FIRST

Do you know what happens when you love something? You take care of it. When you love your dog, you feed him, talk silly to him and forgive him when he sneaks food off the counter. When you love your home, you take pride in it, keep up with repairs, and feel safe in it. When you love your body, you'll give it better food, exercise, and grace for all its imperfections. When you love yourself despite your shortcomings, the hard work you put in will feel like a gift to yourself, instead of a chore.

It's hard to take care of something you don't love. When you don't like your home, the layout, the needed repairs, the neighbors, all of it starts to deflate you and you stop putting in the effort that's required.

As I tried to explain this concept to my teenage daughters, they gave me insight on one common reason it's so hard to love yourself. To many, it feels arrogant. People assume if you love yourself as you are, then you're proclaiming you're good enough and ignoring your flaws. But loving yourself doesn't deny the flaws, it accepts them while you work on them. We also assume that if we love something, it must fit other people's standards. We don't have to fit anyone standards, including our own, or wait for others to love us first. Loving yourself doesn't tell others that they need to love you, but it does send the message you deserve to be respected because you are no longer tolerating anything less.

You're the only one who needs to love you – your body, your choices, your talents, and every other aspect of your life. For others, they are the only ones who need to love themselves.

WHO SAYS YOU HAVE FLAWS?

In college, I had a professor who hit us with a question that silenced the classroom. My major was Early Childhood Education and the topic was on teaching children with disabilities. She gave us multiple scenarios of what we may encounter and asked us which disabilities were considered normal and could be mainstreamed in the classroom. We shouted out specific disabilities and diagnoses assuming we nailed the answer.

Then she asked, "Who defines normal?"

Stunned, I realized it's our human nature to put a label on everything – normal, pretty, fit, smart, stupid. We need these words to communicate with others, but who determines what is classified as each? As you think about your flaws, who decided it was a flaw? Society may post pictures of similar-looking women on billboards, but as you look around the streets, you quickly become aware of how different everyone looks. Chances are you defined your own flaws by comparing yourself to another. Which means – you don't even have flaws.

Love yourself. Once you do, deciding the best way to take care of yourself will be easy.

THE MANTRA

It may take time to truly learn to love some parts, but I turn it into a phrase that I repeat until I believe it. Then I add a plan to ensure I take action.

For Example:

I love my: car **despite** the scratches and the ugly interior, **not because** it's the new Tesla I'm hoping to get one day.

Because I love it, I am going to: continue to take care of it inside and out, because this will be the stepping stone to get me closer to the next car.

I love my: my marriage **despite** the difficulties we are having right now, **not because** we have it figured out yet.

Because I love it, I am going to: work on listening more and trying to understand what my spouse needs. It may feel like a one-way street, but I am going to give 100% effort to make things work.

I am going to love them passionately enough to make the changes needed.

I love my: life **despite** the anxiety I feel going to my job, **not because** I have my career figured out.

Because I love it, I am going to: give the job I have my best effort. This work ethic I'm practicing will ensure I'm ready and deserving when the next opportunity comes along. In the meantime, I'll also network to let others know what I'm looking for.

Use this exercise to cement the things you already love and encourage the things that still need more work.

I love my _____ despite _____

_____

Not because _____

Because I love it, I am going to: _____

_____

I love my _____ despite _____

_____

Not because _____

Because I love it, I am going to: _____

_____

I love my _____ despite _____

_____

Not because _____

Because I love it, I am going to: _____

_____

I love my _____ despite _____

_____

Not because _____

Because I love it, I am going to: _____

_____

Engrain this go-to phrase in your brain. When you start to wish you were healthier or can't wait until you get a nicer car, remember to love who you are and what you have right now, despite how far you may be from what you think will make you happier. Not only will you grow a spirit of gratitude and appreciation, you'll learn to take better care of what you have. Taking better care of yourself will lead you to your goals faster and give you more peace and contentment while you get there.

10

Betting on Yourself

With a six-month-old in one hand and a pregnancy stick in the other, I walked out of the bathroom in a daze. This was not planned, yet we're all old enough to understand how it happened. Even with no one else to blame, I couldn't seem to pull myself together. I adjusted my elastic pants, stared at those pink lines, and muttered, "At least I'm not out of my maternity clothes yet. I won't have to change my wardrobe."

Just as we found out about this surprise, I mean blessing, things began slowing down at my job. I was working as a loan processor at the time, managing the paperwork for four loan officers. We had no idea we were entering what would later be referred to as 'a housing crisis,' 'the Great Recession,' and an overall bad economic time for many.

Concerned about my job security, I spent any extra time at work trying to help the loan officers on my team market themselves in order to generate more business. I tried to make myself more valuable, but volume continued to decrease and I knew I was the lowest-salaried person on the totem pole.

To be proactive, I went to my boss and made a proposition. "What if you paid me a commission instead of a salary?" He looked a little confused, yet was intrigued enough to allow me to share the details. Pointing out how things had slowed down, I offered to sacrifice my salary and only take a paycheck when a loan from my team closed. My monthly income would be directly tied to sales production, so if my team wasn't making money – neither would I. This would drive me to help increase volume, boost company profits, and in turn, provide me with more job security and a higher income potential if the company began doing well again.

On top of that, I hated the idea of losing this job. It was a fantastic environment. I was surrounded by great people who had become good friends, and I was constantly being challenged. It was everything I wanted. But somehow, even that early in my career, I knew steady income didn't mean security. If my department didn't have the business to support the number of employees we had, someone had to go. Even though I'd been there for four years, I was still a newbie compared to the rest.

My boss told me not to worry, that there was no reason to believe my position would be eliminated. He had been through highs and lows before and just needed to get the sales team motivated to bring in more business.

Relieved and pregnant, I jumped right back into work. From going above and beyond in customer service to cleaning the office, I challenged myself to be the best employee I could possibly be. Although my position had been deemed safe, I knew that wasn't permission to slack off.

But as business continued to decline, I couldn't shake the feeling I needed to be more proactive. The magnitude of this housing crash and recession were beginning to show, and other banks in the industry were starting rounds of layoffs. So, I went back to my boss and offered to take on any additional roles that would benefit the company. I made a second proposition which included reducing my salary, becoming a licensed loan officer, and bringing in my own business to supplement my income.

Again, he assured me I had nothing to worry about.

Four months into my pregnancy, my boss called me into his office – TO LAY ME OFF! I sat there stunned. I was struggling to adjust to an infant at home, dealing with exhaustion from the pregnancy, and now this!? Although his news shouldn't have come as a surprise, after spending the last several months being proactive, I was devastated. After presenting multiple options that would have justified my employment and could have potentially increased business, this news still gutted me. I cycled through hurt, anger, shock, and worry about what would happen next for my family financially.

At home with Scott, I cried. And cried and cried. We sat on the couch, and I unloaded all my frustrations and emotions. I let it all out. When I finally stopped whining about the injustice, I felt this crazy sense of peace. It was a calm mixed with fire and determination. I wiped away my tears and said, "You know, I can't help but wonder if this is meant to be a good thing. I feel like I can get further by betting on myself rather than trusting any company."

The next day, I asked for another meeting and told my boss I wanted to be a full-time commissioned loan officer. I would stay, but give up any salary. He agreed, which really irritated me since I had expressed interest in sales prior to the layoff, but nevertheless, I knew it was the right move. The amazing people I worked with were the right ones to teach me the ropes. My husband was able to get insurance through his part-time job despite being a student at the time, and although we had no idea if and when my next paycheck would arrive, we just kept moving forward. I got started right away.

TAKING CHANCES

Any time I received a lead, I snuck into the conference room so no one could hear me fumble around on the phone. Sitting with my back to the glass doors, I hid both my trembling hands and the tears streaming down my face as I made each call. Here I was, betting on myself, and a phone call felt like jumping out of a perfectly good airplane. Ironic, huh? I reached a lot of voicemails (thankfully) but did have a few people take time to scream and swear at me before they hung up. After each call, I would take a deep breath, give myself a pep talk, then slowly dial the next number.

Throughout the months before Hannah was born, I continued to make phone calls. Although I was still extremely anxious, I eventually stopped taking the no's so personally and even began making calls at my desk – without tears. I put some flyers together to network, showing up at open houses and realtor offices. I may have sat in the car hyperventilating before gaining the courage to open the door, but I learned to walk into businesses to promote myself anywhere that could help generate new sales.

Within two months, I had $10,000 of potential income waiting in the loans I had originated!

None of them closed, and I made zero.

Unfortunately, I lacked the experience to know what initial questions to ask potential clients. I was so excited for any loan I could get my hands on that I didn't do enough research to make sure I could close it!

I didn't make a dime before Hannah was born.

After her birth I kept at it, working a flexible schedule while raising two babies. Income began trickling in slowly, but I was still angry. A couple of co-workers asked why I had become a loan officer, so I explained about the layoff and how I felt this was a good move for me. When they asked our boss about it, he denied all of it. Another shock, and another reason to listen to my instincts telling me to go.

I knew if I was really going to bet on myself, I'd have to bet bigger.

I had one last meeting with my boss, and this time there was no fear or concern. My confidence led the conversation: "When I was earning a salary, I did my job as I was told. Now that I'm working for commission, I have to treat this like my own business, and I don't think this is a fit. I need to move on." The conversation lasted a couple more minutes, and shortly after Hannah was born, I moved on to my next commissioned loan officer job.

Although I knew I was the only one responsible for my future, it helped finding a company that aligned with the same values and provided the resources needed for success. It took a couple of moves before I found a company with that kind of culture – one that helped me do things I didn't know I could do. They encouraged me to constantly challenge myself. I set massive goals that were almost too embarrassing to share. Some might have called them arrogant. My new boss not only helped our team believe we could set such lofty goals; he also provided the resources to make that happen.

The money I made over the next few years would have taken me the rest of my career to earn had I stayed comfortable.

I bet on myself and I won, big, over time. To me, a salary had become equal to *no* job security, which tends to be the opposite of popular opinion. But when someone else pays your salary, they have the power to choose how much and for how long. When I'm paying their salary, I don't have to live in fear of the highs and the lows. I know that if I do a good job and still lose my job through no fault of my own, it's much easier to land my next one as long as I'm willing to continue to bet on myself.

COMMON MISCONCEPTIONS

As I type this, signs of another recession linger like a dark cloud. Some economists tell us to expect it and others say it won't happen – half will be right. Your opinion may be based on your industry surroundings. Over the past three years, we've seen interest rates hit record lows, only to watch them quickly shoot back up as the Federal Reserve looks to slow down inflation and the rise of housing prices.

Fear of this crisis has led to massive layoffs, mergers, and closings. Tens of thousands have been impacted and still struggle to find work. The ripple effect impacts numerous industries, and since I'm connected to so many real estate professionals on LinkedIn, my feed was filled with shouts of doom and gloom.

Some have been out of work for months, and with unemployment running out, they are falling behind on bills. It's heartbreaking. But more heartbreaking are the posts closed-minded to certain opportunities, begging others to stop reaching out with sales jobs or business opportunities as they refused to entertain variable income. Many shared their anger at the offers. Most said they needed security in a salary, yet they didn't see – it was the salary that had made their job so insecure.

Many of us have been, or could end up, in circumstances that force us to take the first job that comes along. Without a safety net, if you're the sole provider with other mouths to feed, desperation may lead the charge in decision-making. Unfortunately, that same desperation may lead to frantic decisions and missed opportunities.

When we become fixated on what resources we think we need, we miss what's available to us. Many incentive-based positions may offer a guaranteed salary along with commissions and bonuses. Others may provide a twelve-month guarantee of income as you train and start growing your business.

If you want to give it a shot, but don't think you have what it takes, remember – skills can be learned. Most business owners and salespeople don't start as experts. Instead, they may have a couple strong qualities, inspiring the confidence in themselves to go out on their own and learn the rest.

When I encourage colleagues to bet on themselves, I always answer the one question most never think to ask – how many loans do I need to close each month to meet my current earnings? When they realize it's more attainable than imagined, they get their first boost of confidence.

The same can be asked in any industry. How many copiers do I need to sell to make what I earn as secretary? How many web pages do I need to build to match my salary as an assistant? How many accounts do I need to manage?

After Hannah was born, I worked just a little each day. After three p.m., I only took important calls, leaving the rest until the next day. Even with reduced hours, it didn't take long for my commission to beat my old salary.

Whether you're tumbling to rock bottom or not, it's always best to choose questions over assumptions when it comes to any offers in your career.

SUCCESS STORIES

Lisa

Every once in a while, a team member fits so well, you do everything you can to hold on to them. For years, Lisa was my assistant. Fantastic at her job, she helped elevate my business to multiple levels during our time together. Driven and excited about our success, she took ownership of her role. Unfortunately for me, her ambition fed her curiosity about sales. For my own sake, I wanted to dissuade her, but I know supporting anyone willing to bet on themselves will always be the way to go. Reluctantly, I warned her of the highs and lows, then stepped back to watch her shine.

Shine she did. She multiplied her income during those first years and quickly became an established, reputable addition to the industry. Lisa loved the stability of a steady paycheck, but the possibility of exceeding the bi-weekly status-quo was more thrilling. She now controls her financial outcome, so her family has been able to take more trips, and live where and how they want.

Jim

Getting the offer of a lifetime, Jim was faced with a tough decision. This was everything others told him he wanted, but he was struggling to buy into this golden opportunity – a hefty salary, incomparable benefits, and a hiring manager who already knew and trusted his work. This would set his family up exponentially compared to where they were. The problem? Jim couldn't sleep the night before he needed to accept the offer. He had no peace.

When he talked with his wife, she confirmed what he knew deep down. If this job didn't feel right, it was time for him to start his own business. That was over twenty years ago, and he still talks about the journey. Not all his stories are of success, but he's never regretted taking that chance on himself. It gave him the adventure and fulfillment he longed for.

Lynne

Lynne defied conventional wisdom in landing her next role. Looking through the classifieds and playing the waiting game didn't work for her. She hit the streets and twice walked into businesses that showed no signs of hiring. Twice, she nailed on-the-spot interviews.

Both companies were looking to expand, but neither had the opportunity to post the position yet. Nevertheless, Lynne was offered both roles, which gave her the chance to be picky.

Most job seekers will apply, wait, and hope. Lynne knew what she had to offer and took the initiative to design her own life.

Jennifer

When Jennifer walks into a room asking for attention, everyone stops to give it. Not out of fear, but out of a desire to support their leader in her requests. They know she's second-in-command when it comes to running the company, so if she has a question about the balance sheet or projected sales, the answer is provided as quickly as possible.

Now in her forties, Jennifer still reminisces about her first days on the job – as a sixteen-year-old who cleaned the very offices she runs today! She spent over twenty-five years asking questions and learning about every department as she rose through the ranks. The bet she made started with the trust she had in herself to show the company she was the person they needed.

BETTING ON STRESS

Two things that generally come with higher income potential are more stress and greater responsibility – another reason many avoid betting on themselves. They aren't sure if they can handle the pressure, yet the stress many strive to avoid tends to be self-generated. When starting out in a new role, we easily become overwhelmed managing everything on our plate. We concern ourselves with things that haven't happened yet, allowing worry to drain us.

Managing this stress takes training and practice over time. That's where the disciplines I added into my life helped. When I started in sales, I felt significant stress even though I only had one loan in my pipeline. Filled with worry, I had to monitor my single loan, continue to find new business, manage the house and kids, and keep our finances in the black. When I closed five loans in a month, I was sure I had reached my max.

Today, thanks to the work I've done on becoming my best future self, I've easily closed over seventy loans in a single month. I grew into that capability not just by developing my work skills, but by growing as a person who could balance more on my plate without any additional effort.

To start adding more responsibility, I had to remove unnecessary emotions that took too much time and energy. Things like worry, fear, and doubt that were sucking the life from me. I woke up panicked about things that might happen:

What if I can't get through my to-do list?

What if an appraisal comes in low?

What if an upset client calls today?

What if a client cancels their loan?

What if that loan doesn't get approved?

I wasted so much valuable time worrying about the what-ifs. On the rare occasion one of these things actually did happen, I jumped into action and took care of it. Fixing the problem took a moment. Worrying about it was consuming hours.

In order to conquer worry, determine your 'what if' stressors and defeat them with the truth. For example:

Stress: What if I can't get through my to-do list?

Truth: I can finish the rest tomorrow. If I can't get to all my clients, I will message them to let them know when I'll reach out. There are only a couple of errands that need done today, so I'll knock them out in the morning to get them out of the way. There are days things are slow and I miss this chaos, so embrace the suck!

Stress: What if Bob's appraised value comes in low?

Truth: Then I'll tell him. I can't control how he responds, but how I handle it reveals my character. The value may even come in higher! I won't think about it another minute until the appraisal is here.

Stress: What if an upset client calls today?

Truth: Let them vent. Listen to their needs and try to rectify the situation. If you can't find a solution, it's okay to admit the deal may not work, but most people just want to be heard. Don't shy away from tough conversations and treat their concerns with respect.

Next, give yourself grace if something goes wrong. Some days the house won't get clean, you'll forget to call a client, or fail to pack your child's lunch. It's okay. You've become relatable! Do what you can and move on.

DROP TIME-CONSUMING EMOTIONS

If you struggle with stress in your current job to the point it impacts your personal life, first, identify unnecessary emotions taking up space and draining your energy. Quitting your job won't fix your relationship with your feelings. You might need a new position, but if it's your emotions getting the best of you, they will follow you to your next environment if they remain uncontrolled.

When making decisions from your highest and best self, you can bet on that stress. Let it come. Show it what you've got and let it know you can control it. Those who can handle more can be given more, and more opportunities lead to more rewards.

If you're in an environment with unhealthy expectations and deadlines, journaling and meditation won't just help you navigate your feelings; they'll also show you when it's time for change. It's one thing to learn to dominate the stress in your life, it's another to endure harassment or bullying. If your mindset isn't the problem, it may be time to run!

You'll find many positions that require high stress and responsibility for less pay or opportunity. Instead of jumping to find a job with less stress, bet on yourself. Find a job that pays more for the same stress, then learn to get it under control.

YOU WILL BE UNCOMFORTABLE – CHOOSE WHEN

"Be uncomfortable now to live comfortably later."

– Unknown

"Live like no one else so later you can live like no one else"

– Dave Ramsey

"Don't give up what you most want for what you want now"

– Richard G Scott

"If you aim at nothing, you will hit it every time"

– Zig Ziglar

So many variations of the same thing, yet equally important. What you do today determines how you'll live later. Many people stay in their comfort zone during the hustle phase of life. When they have the most energy – and yes, likely the most responsibility – they play it safe, looking for a secure job they could lose at any time. They accumulate debt because it's easier than saying no. They won't do more work than necessary and have no aspirations to advance. They don't invest, they don't take risks, and they don't learn new things.

Does that sound comfortable? Many of you just cringed. You already know how that story ends. Perhaps, you lived that scenario and are waking up to the harsh reality that staying comfortable in your hustling years means you're now uncomfortable in your reflective years. The debt didn't automatically go away. The savings didn't magically accrue like you expected, and all those risks you avoided have paid off for the people around you. Or maybe, you hustled for years, but had a setback caused by illness, divorce, or another emergency.

No matter where you are today, your next move is just a series of small decisions that lead you closer to comfort.

We recently had a fantastic tenant who began to fall behind on his rent. He went from being a stellar occupant to engaging in a he-said, she-said battle with his partner that led to police reports, possible eviction, and risk of termination from his employer.

His domestic battles poured into every aspect of his life, and it was spiraling out of control. We spoke to him about his discomfort and explained his two options: he could stop paying rent, avoid our calls, and face an eviction, or he could communicate with us to work out a deal that released him from his obligations with no additional consequence.

This tenant felt understandably uncomfortable regardless of his next move. He dreaded every conversation with us, but realized each decision was a choice that would lead him closer to relief or deeper into ruin. By dealing with, instead of avoiding, he escaped with minimal consequence.

LISTEN TO THE IDEAS

Learning to bet on yourself doesn't necessarily mean a change in the way you get paid. I focused earlier on transitioning into a commission or self-employed role, but you may have a career you enjoy which comes with stability, a consistent salary, and is exactly what you want. I would never ask a teacher who believes in what they do to start their own business, but there are still numerous ways to bet on yourself. Are you investing properly or avoiding the topic because it's not in your wheelhouse? Maybe you'd love to purchase a couple of rental properties and pay them off before you retire? Can you sell your lesson plans to other teachers online?

No matter what it looks like in your life, ask yourself how you can spend the next several years a bit uncomfortable so you can live more comfortably later.

Don't ignore those ideas that pop into your head, or hobbies you'd like to pursue. Is there something you'd like to create and sell for a little extra cash, or take on as a personal challenge? Do it. Do it before that nasty voice in your brain tells you it's a bad idea or gives you an excuse.

Don't judge yourself if you start them all but finish none. Be open to each idea until one gets you so excited you can't get it out of your head. If you have a finishing problem, seek resources. Accountability partners or networking groups can give guidance and help you overcome obstacles. Allow yourself to make mistakes and fumble your way through something you've never done before. Be kind to yourself. That negative voice may tell you, "You can't do it" or "It's a silly idea," so you'll need to train it like you trained your emotions. Never talk to yourself in a way you wouldn't tolerate from others. Give the voice of positivity more time, effort, and respect. It knows what you are capable of.

I started betting on myself years ago, but I'm still learning how to fully take advantage of what that means. Looking back on the last twenty years of ideas I never implemented and roles I felt unqualified to ask for, I've decided enough is enough. It's time to stop listening to the excuses and start giving myself reasons why it's going to be awesome!

SHOW UP FOR YOURSELF

When we keep promises to ourselves, we build our self-confidence. If you've never finished anything or hit a goal, your confidence in achieving your goal may be pretty low, which is why it's important to celebrate small victories. Those little victories are the steps you use to build your confidence and keep you motivated.

Do you want to write your own book, but worry about having enough ideas? Don't wait until you're finished to begin celebrating. When you hit five pages, celebrate. When you finish the first chapter, party again. Allow yourself to be excited with what you've accomplished and determine your next milestone.

Thinking about the end result of our efforts can be overwhelming. If you told me today my future includes a best-selling book, speaking gigs, and an interview with Oprah, I would lose myself trying to please the masses instead of writing what I'm led to say. Instead, I just keep taking each step, never sure of how the future will unfold. I can only see as far as my next word, but somehow, the words keep showing up. I have faith they'll continue to appear until I look back and am wowed by how much I've accomplished.

Knowing our future would cause us to lose the future we're capable of.

When the project is complete and the results still aren't where you had hoped them to be, don't get discouraged. Continue showing up day after day, and don't ignore new ideas that come to mind. If you believe there is something bigger than you, then you can trust it to lead you down a path you can't see yourself.

Betting on yourself also takes the power of creating your life from others and puts it back into your own hands. No one else is responsible for your future. In an average life span, you will have approximately thirty-eight years of Republicans running the country and thirty-eight years of Democrats. You may like one set of thirty-eight over the other, but at the end of the day, you are responsible for your life during all seventy-six years. Are you going to spend half your life angry, blaming the political administration for your mediocrity, or are you going to use each administration's flaws and strengths to your advantage?

You also control your paycheck and growth. If you do the bare minimum at work, expect the bare minimum in return. If you're tired of always being micromanaged and undervalued, create a plan to become your own boss or move on to a place that appreciates your talents and compensates you for them. Those places exist, but they generally hire people who have confidence in themselves and aren't afraid to take calculated risks.

DON'T HATE THE PLAYER, TRY THE GAME

When the company's top producer walks by your office, how do you react? Are you angry about the money they make? Are you jealous because you lack the same charisma or skills? Have you ever disliked someone because you felt they acted like they were better than you, but, if you were completely honest, you really just struggle watching them enjoy their life while you sit on the bench? You're the one who suffers when you see others from a bitter perspective.

People are attracted to like-minded people. When you think others aren't making an effort to connect with you, they may actually be avoiding the attitudes that bring them down.

I hate to break it to you, but the successful business owner or salesperson doesn't worry about what you think. They may be empathetic, but they aren't in their office lowering their sales goals or profit projections to make you feel better about where you are in life. Instead of being angry or jealous – join them.

In 2011, the Occupy Wall Street movement came to life. People were angry about income inequality and corporate corruption and protested in New York's Financial District. The protest lasted weeks and dominated the news. There was a lot of talk about the 'one-percenters,' which represented the top one percent of income earners in the US. The talk centered around their greed and blatant disregard for the working class. I understand greed and corruption exist in abundance, but many of the business owners and CEOs I know in this income bracket are good people who care deeply about their contribution to society. They donate to charities. They care about their business' reputation and value their employees. I decided to strive to become a one-percenter to use my wealth for good, instead of wasting my time angry at the ones who had made it.

The next time you find yourself looking at the financially successful with disdain, ask yourself why. If they're unethical, condescending, cheaters and liars, I don't blame you for not liking those specific individuals. But if they appear to be decent humans with flaws, ask yourself if you would feel any different if you removed their successes and achievements.

They bet on themselves once and continue to do so daily. What could you do if you tried the same?

11

GET READY FOR WHAT YOU DON'T HAVE... YET

Although this chapter came during a time when opening social media shows a discouraging number of people sharing news of their recent layoff, unexpected job loss can impact anyone at any time. When the global pandemic arrived in the U.S. in 2020, over forty percent of Americans lost their job – at least temporarily. Many industries experienced a surge in business, but are now feeling the repercussions as the market cools off. Tens of thousands in mortgage and real estate have been negatively impacted over the last year, as well as 12,000 from Google, 18,000 from Amazon, and 10,000 from Microsoft in January alone.

People are scared and broken, struggling to find their next position and pay bills as companies slow hiring or receive hundreds of resumes for a single job posting.

Although I refuse to get caught in the rabbit hole of doom and gloom, I check the news each day to remain empathetic to what others are going through. I've shared the story of my layoff and still vividly remember that pain and fear.

These layoffs bring big emotions. Some blame the companies for their poor decision making and putting profits first. Recruiters get blasted for the way they do, or don't, communicate. Scammers play on others' misfortune, offering jobs that don't exist in order to steal an applicant's personal information. On the flip side, good people are stepping up to facilitate introductions and sharing job openings for those who need it.

Many of those entering unforeseen unemployment loved their role and brought their best selves to work each day. Others felt trapped and dreaded each day they showed up. No matter which end of the spectrum one may be on, both sets of job seekers include those who waited until the layoff to prepare themselves for potential change.

PREPARING FOR TOMORROW

It begs the question – how are you preparing today to get ready for your next role – whether unexpected or not? We both know you are going to turn up that smile and charm for an hour to dominate your interview, but what happens the hours after that? Have you been preparing for this role the last two days or the last two years? If you land this new position, you will still be the same person. Does that person gossip, complain, and avoid working a minute past their allotted hours? Or has that person been building their best self, preparing for any obstacles or opportunities life will throw at them?

A new job doesn't make a new you. It may feel like a fresh start and chance to start over, but your current self will eventually be the one showing up.

When I was in my early twenties, I held an entry-level job at a car dealership during college. A few of us girls became good friends, but we were anything but good influences on each other. We would get together after work and hit the bars, act like idiots, and talk about each other's behavior the next day – behind each other's back. We would talk about co-workers and complain about the company, yet, we would also do thorough work and treat clients with care, causing us to believe we deserved raises and recognition. We didn't realize what a disruption we were each day.

After college, I landed my first "real" job – one with benefits and a 401k. I was ready to put my childish behavior behind me but, it was only a matter of time before I found the like-minded co-workers. We hung out during lunch to gossip, complain, and share our disappointment about the raises and recognition we weren't getting. No matter the quality of my work, I couldn't get ahead. Deep down I knew why, so I finally started shedding my poor behavior, connected with the people who challenged me to do better, and worked on being the leader I had the potential to be – long before I had any sort of leadership position.

As new opportunities present themselves, I continue to challenge myself to prepare for the next. Maybe it's another job, maybe it's a new hobby, or maybe it's time to guide others through their journey. No matter what, I am constant preparation mode.

While I believe in saying yes to the amazing job you may not feel ready for, you likely won't receive an offer if you aren't showing the potential in your current role. Those who believe they could be a leader if they were just given the chance won't be chosen for the role if they haven't been developing the necessary skills in advance. Some think a new job that excites them will give them the energy to go all day, but they may not be viewed as energetic enough to land the position.

ENERGY MATTERS

Consider the 4 Areas of Life. Have you been developing healthy habits so you can work in high energy mode each day, or does your production decrease every afternoon? If you're looking to move up internally, the decision makers have already been watching you. Externally, many can feel your energy in an interview and tell if you're losing momentum. The person that wins will be the person who's been preparing for years.

In a competitive market, employers are looking for more than just skills. They are looking for the person who brings positive energy to the office and wants to get better every day. Employers need staff with already established discipline and accountability to add to the culture they are trying to build.

One day, a new role will present itself whether it's working for someone else or for yourself. You'll find yourself with opportunities to gain new relationships and manage more assets. There'll be an obstacle to overcome or a competitive market you need to stand out in to win.

Are you getting ready now?

Is your energy in the optimum position?

Are you open to new things?

Are you ready to show up again and again even when the environment doesn't excite you?

Can you influence the environment yourself?

DON'T TELL PEOPLE WHO YOU ARE – BE WHO YOU ARE

As I connect with friends impacted by reductions in staffing, I hear a theme – "I'm going to stay positive", or "I'm a positive person."

Everyone wants to be positive and many claim to be so. Everyone wants to be kind, trustworthy, and honest. But are you? And if you truly are, an announcement becomes unnecessary. A beautiful person doesn't – or shouldn't – announce their beauty. If they are truly beautiful by someone else's definition of beauty, they will be seen as such.

Shortly after the birth of Finley and my decision to skip maternity leave, the company I worked for was sold. A company I loved and anticipated staying at for years. In an effort to persuade us to take a lower compensation plan, the new owners sent a non-experienced representative to plead their case. His brilliant plan was to tell me I should just take the pay cut because I wasn't necessary. He informed me that no other company would pay me as much and I should be thankful to even have a job. Not a recommended approach. The annual numbers came out and I was in the top 1% of loan officers in the nation and #2 in the state. Not exactly an "anyone can do it" record-breaking year.

I knew his words were wrong, but they don't just go away. They ate at me. They weren't just the words of one man, they represented the culture of the new ownership.

As this battle went on, I lost motivation and became consumed by these words that hurt me so much. When I thought about my future with another company, it was coming from a place of vengeance, no longer excitement for my next chapter.

At the time, I met with a mentor once a month, and I unloaded all of this pretty passionately. I explained that one moment I was excited and ready to push forward and the next, I was broken and hurt. These emotions rotated on a continuous cycle, draining me of my energy and focus.

Then she broke the news. She told me that I can't be angry and excited at the same time.

"Wait, what?" I questioned.

She went on to explain that you can't have two emotions at the same time so when I was truly excited for my future, I couldn't be bitter in that moment, and vice versa. She gave me permission to feel any emotion, but I had to choose when I would give my time to each.

This gave me an idea that allowed me to stay centered while feeling the negative emotions that come up. During my work day, I focused on hitting my goals and being the best I could be, even if I planned to leave. During my workouts, I allowed myself to feel angry, yell, cry, and embrace any emotion that arose. In that hour, I was a mess. I ran faster and pushed harder, but after a few weeks, I regained my strength and grew tired of wasting my gym time being angry. I didn't want to cry anymore. I didn't want to let the bitterness impact my ability to do my job, which impacts my paycheck, which impacts my family.

Because I didn't ignore my negativity, I stopped draining myself of hours-long battles cycling through emotions. I just gave it a short period of time daily where it couldn't interrupt anything important in my life.

If you are one of the tens of thousands laid off, feel what you need to feel, but pick the times you are going to feel it so it doesn't consume you, interrupt quality time with others, or slow work that still needs to get done. Being angry or depressed is an understandable emotion during this time, but it won't hurt your prior employer, it will hurt you. Your new potential employer may even pick up on the hurt, anger, and blame and choose a different candidate. When my numbers started decreasing after that meeting, my company didn't panic. They just believed I was proving them right as I was making myself replaceable. I refused to let them be right. I proved I was necessary – then left when it was the right time for me to go.

Feel what you need to feel, but control what you feel. Your character doesn't need a social media announcement. If you are trustworthy, your integrity will show. If you are positive, people will see it in the way you react to the trials in your life.

On that job interview, find ways to show who you are without announcing it. Your potential employer may ask you to describe yourself, but instead of adjectives, give examples. Want to say you're high-energy? Tell them about your hiking excursions. You're hard-working? Everyone thinks they are. What makes you stand out above the rest? Provide examples of your work ethic.

No matter your current employment situation, start preparing yourself today for your potential and opportunity tomorrow. As much as I'd like to tell you that companies shouldn't undervalue you, lay you off, or treat your poorly, that will always be a possibility. The burden of responsibility to take care of you is on *you*. If you didn't think they cared when you were there, it won't get better when you're gone. Get yourself in the best position to be ready for anything at all times.

12

TWO SIDES OF FEAR

"When you're 20 you care what everyone thinks.
When you're 40 you stop caring what everyone thinks.
When you're 60 you realize no one was ever thinking about
you in the first place."

– Unknown

December is my favorite time of year. For many, it's the sparkling Christmas lights, quality time with family, or the smell of cinnamon sticks and sugar cookies. For me, it's a time of reflection and preparation for the following year. I can't wait to set goals and list all I'd like to accomplish in the new year. Many items get carried over from the past twelve months, like the disciplines and random acts of kindness, but the career goals require a lot of planning and commitment.

I always loved setting unrealistic goals for my job, but the last few years, it's getting harder. I can't seem to come up with anything that brings me any sort of excitement. The career goals usually revolve around closing loans, but I'm getting tired of the same old. Being a loan officer is safe – it's what I know. Although I still enjoy it, I feel the burden of all the other endeavors I've been avoiding sitting on my chest.

After all I've said in this book about identifying feelings, it's pretty obvious something is telling me that I need to explore new paths.

Listening to this voice scares me. What else would I do? What if I just need to keep pushing? So many questions and concerns, but it's been obvious for a while that it's time to take some risks and try new things.

So what kept me from any sort of change? The obvious answer was fear. But fear of what? Failure? Starting over? Running out of money? A lot of journaling revealed that I cared too much about what people think. It was that simple. I was okay with the risks and a potential failure, but I couldn't stop worrying about what others would think if I did fall short. I was afraid they thought my ideas were silly or too ill-planned to finish. The judgement of others prevented me from trying new things.

Knowing I squashed numerous ideas or skipped out on potential experiences because of these fears is an awful realization. I avoided advertising my business on social media to keep from annoying people, despite the potential it had to further support my family. I ignored countless opportunities that excited me to prevent others from seeing me as a novice. I put off writing this book for eight years because I was too embarrassed for people to hear my thoughts.

I needed to make a change. I could no longer allow the fear of others' opinions hinder me from participating in my own life to the fullest. Especially since those very same people didn't even know or care what I was up to! Everything changed when I asked myself one question:

What could I accomplish if I didn't give a shit what people thought?

This question fired me up. When I stepped on the other side of fear and made a list of everything I could achieve if I didn't care about others, it was astounding. I saw things I always thought would be cool, and activities I fantasized about trying, but never had the guts to do.

FINDING THE OTHER SIDE OF FEAR

I began to imagine a line of fear running through the middle of my life. On the left, I listed all of the things fear of that line kept me from doing. I avoided that line like a bug who knows if you get too close, you'll get zapped. I didn't want to end up knocked around, paralyzed, or even worse. Not living your life to the fullest can feel like your soul is getting crushed. Ironically, by not crossing that line, the same is already happening slowly and painfully.

Have you been there? You may already be feeling the way that line steals your joy, or it may be years until you wake up and realize all you lost by never crossing over. Either way, staying to the left of that line hurts.

Using the diagram below, I was unstoppable. The list on the right became so amazing to me, I had no other option than to make choices from that column. If anyone laughed or judged, that was okay, I'd move them to the left side and continue connecting with those on the right. What I found was that no one needed moved to the left because they are all too busy working on their own lives and happy to support mine. My fears were all fabricated.

Limits and regrets created by not crossing the line of fear		Everything I could do if I didn't care about other's opinions
~I will never put my thoughts on paper to inspire others to live their best life ~I will hold myself back in branding myself and my business which will delay hitting financial goals ~I won't grow or inspire others ~I will lose my passion for chasing my dreams if I never chase them ~I will die writing mortgage loans even though there are other things I really want to try ~I will grow old full of regrets ~I'll be mediocre or average ~I will realize the people I was intimidated by never even thought about me, yet they took up space in my head ~I will have wasted my one life sitting on the sidelines	FEAR OF WHAT OTHER PEOPLE WILL THINK	~I could write a book and brand myself, inspire others, and learn new things about myself ~I could end up a best-seller, a speaker, a mentor or more. ~I could end up meeting people that have an influence in my life in ways I can't predict ~I can follow each new challenge and create a passionate life ~This experience will teach me that I can do things I haven't dreamed yet if I ignore the voices that don't matter ~Everything and anything is possible and open to me ~I can look back and know I lived life to the absolute fullest ~I could teach my daughters to live the life they want to live by showing them how

The list on the left held big disappointment. Worse, it's where I'd been hanging out. The list on the right still gives me butterflies and doesn't truly reflect how big I see my potential. This column shows me the tenacious force I can become on the other side of fear. When I consider the possibilities, I realize I haven't begun to identify everything I'm capable of after I cross that line. That's what excites and motivates me the most!

In the few weeks since I've completed this exercise, I still find myself being drawn to the left of fear. When I am hesitant to speak up or try something new, I ask myself two questions: Which side of fear I am standing on? And what could I succeed in doing if I didn't care what people thought? Then I take the action needed to cross that line and become an unrelenting force.

Despite the short time I've spent here, I've discovered playing on that right side of fear is a lot more fun. Concern about what I'm going to regret not doing in my life has vanished because I'm too busy doing it now. Any time fear revisits while I'm taking new risks, I grab a pen and paper and list my likely regrets on the left and unlimited potential on the right until it feels like the right side is too amazing to deny.

How will you feel when you look back on your life? What fears stop you from being all that you can be? Are you stuck in a job you hate because you're afraid to risk the financial security? Do you spend so much time worrying about your finances or your weight that you can't enjoy what you do have? Is it time to work past the dread and have tough conversations with your partner?

The unknown holds a lot of fear, but being brave and finding out leads to a lot of joy.

Take some time to identify your fears and map out what life could look like on the right side of that line. Your answers may start short, but force yourself to dig deeper until you feel you've explored everything holding you back and identified all of your potential. Then soak in the feeling of each. Imagine the discouragement living on the left and the power of moving to the right of fear. Take pleasure in the amazement knowing you can step over this line any minute and live an abundant and passionate life you hadn't realized was possible.

THAT VOICE

"Who do you talk to most every single day?" I asked.

"You, dad, my teacher, my friends," Hannah guessed the answer I was looking for.

"Nope. Yourself. You can't escape that voice in your head. Have you ever stopped to listen to what it is saying? It can be a real jerk."

The hardest part about overcoming your fears and betting on yourself is that voice in your head. When we let it, that voice feeds those fears – *you should be worried about what other people think, they're smarter than you, you can think of new ideas all you want, but you know you won't do anything with them.* Ouch.

When I finally stopped and listened to everything this voice was saying, I realized several things:

- That voice is not nice. I would never let another person spew these ugly words to my face.
- That voice controls my actions when I don't have control of it.
- I need to shut this voice down.

To steal back control, I take immediate action by:

1. Changing any hostile words to something supportive. 'You can't do it' turned into 'this is going to be awesome when I'm done.' Even if I didn't quite believe it, I still chose a kinder replacement.
2. Refuting the lies with facts. When that voice told me I wasn't smart enough or good enough, I responded with

my list of accomplishments. Plus, I reminded the voice that I didn't need to be smart to accomplish something, I just needed to take action.

3.   Reacting as if another person said these things instead of my own voice. If I wouldn't tolerate the words from someone else, I refused to tolerate it from myself.

Not only did I eventually change the way I talked to myself, I set the example for others on how to talk to me. This voice in my head was whirling up fear and giving me reasons to stay average. But the only way to change the narrative was to stop and listen. I assumed that voice knew me well and was pretty reasonable. However, after I paid attention, I realized it sounded like an irrational child who couldn't be reasoned with. Just like a child, training required consistency and discipline. Those negative conversations still creep in, and when they do, I return to the action plan listed above and put the voice back in its place.

Your voice may not be this bold or blunt, but no matter where it is in harshness and volume, it's never too late to coach it to be supportive of all your endeavors. First, let it be heard so you can get a grasp of what it's saying. Do not listen with the intention of believing and accepting it. Listen so you can shut it down and only allow it to speak the kindness and grace you deserve.

If you haven't accepted how amazing you are yet, you may actually regard this voice as truth. Whether you believe this voice speaks fact or opinion, it's time to focus on ensuring you are only receiving the grace and support you deserve. Remember, you are being kind to yourself despite your flaws, not because you've worked them out and have it together. Whether you feel you deserve it or not is irrelevant. Be as kind to yourself as you would another, because kindness is always the better choice.

That voice will attempt to inflate every struggle into an internal attack. A decision over a salad or pizza for dinner can turn to an inner battle over a lifetime of poor eating habits. Even when you make a choice that supports your goals, that voice may tell you that you got lucky this time and speculate on your next failure.

You may not be able to stop the voice from constantly providing an opinion, but you can make sure its opinion is one of encouragement. Your job is not to assess it for accuracy, it's to make sure it stays out of the way if it can't keep up with the person you're becoming.

Before you know it, you'll start to feeling the grace and support you give yourself and believe you're worthy of both. Even the evenings pizza trumps salads (which are plenty at my house), that voice will change from "I knew you couldn't do it" to "pizza sounds great – let's eat!"

THE FORCE FIELD

Eventually, if you let them, your words will grow from cheerleader to new truths about how amazing and capable you are. You may think that sounds arrogant. What will people think if they knew you looked into the mirror and told yourself how awesome you are? Great news! They will never know unless you tell them. They will, however, watch your confidence grow and intuitively know you no longer tolerate anything less than kindness and support in your life.

A force field made up of your energy and confidence will begin to surround you. Others can sense the intensity of your field on any given day. If it's strong and clear, everyone will recognize your confidence cannot be shaken. When they see that force field radiating, they won't waste their time doubting you. They move on to the next person with low energy and start picking at them. It's important to protect your confidence and energy daily.

This voice impacts everyone – women and men, young and old. Some have learned to control it, others claim to be immune to it, and too many succumb to it every day. It can be astonishing when someone you have always viewed as beautiful and having it all opens up about this voice in their head that convinces her she is ugly and a fraud. Your voice always wished you were more like her. Her voice didn't want to be herself.

I don't want any of my daughters to ever tell themselves they are ugly, stupid, or a fraud. But the only way I can truly teach them how to avoid second-guessing their potential is to set the example. They can't walk into a room and hear me mumble how dumb I am for leaving the milk out. They can't see my body slump when I make a mistake. I am open about my struggles, what I do to train the voice and build my force field, but ultimately, it's my actions that demonstrate what I will and will not tolerate in my life.

You are being watched by someone. By everyone. What does your body language tell your co-workers? When you look in the mirror, do your kids notice you sigh and look disappointed at the reflection? Does your boss view your constant negative mumbling as a sign that you aren't ready for new challenges? Your actions are telling others what to think of you because of what you think of yourself.

OWN YOUR LIFE

After you decide what's best for you, take ownership. You may be responsible for other humans, but you now have the tools to weigh the pros and cons to ensure your best interest includes theirs.

You can go after anything you want and you can do it quietly – not because you are worried about what people think, but because you aren't. You can do it as loudly as you'd like also, just do it.

When negative opinions surfaced about how I structured my maternity leave with Finley, I reminded myself those people wouldn't be there to help me anyways. The people who thought I couldn't make it in sales after I got laid off weren't going to pay my bills. Not one coach who expressed frustration with Hannah for choosing another team was paying for her college. Many of the people giving you their two cents have no intention of providing support if you do carry out their unsolicited ideas.

Worse yet, not a single person in any of these scenarios may have even cared. They probably heard your plan, spouted their opinion and didn't think about you again. We take the feedback personally and assume negative intentions. We exaggerate many of these scenarios in our heads and assume others are just as consumed by our decisions as we are. Your name likely isn't coming up at people's dinner table.

This is your life. You only get one. No one but you can be responsible for your success. Look for those people who can provide resources and guidance along the way, but it's up to you to ask for help and seek the resources that improve your life.

IT'S NOT YOUR COMPANY'S RESPONSIBILITY

This also means that your employer is not responsible for your finances. Let that sink in.

That doesn't mean they should get away with bad behavior, but you can't blame them as the reason you aren't where you want to be financially. They offered to pay you a certain wage, and you accepted. Assuming they've honored that, it's up to you to determine what lifestyle that will buy. A respectable employer might give you a raise to keep up with new hires and inflation, but it can't be expected. We would all rather see better budgeting instead of layoffs, but shareholders and bottom lines will always come first. Many companies will recognize good work and reward accordingly, but whether they do or they don't, your life isn't going to stop and wait for your employer to meet your needs.

Before the great recession in 2006, one of my co-workers had been with our company approximately eight years and had gone six of those without a raise. She let the company know she needed a pay increase or would have to look at other employment options. They sent her back to her desk empty-handed.

I called my mom just to check in and share what was going on at my job. I will never forget the conversation.

Me (in exasperated voice): Mom, can you believe it! She's been there eight years and hasn't gotten a raise in years! I can't believe this company. How is she supposed to live off that?!

Mom (calmly): Did they cut her pay?" she questioned.

Me: What? No! Why are you asking? They didn't cut it; they just haven't increased it – in years!

Mom: Then they have kept their end of the bargain. It is up to her to decide what to do next. There is no reason for anyone to be mad at the company. If she's as great as you say she is, it's their loss, but there's nothing anyone should be mad at. Move on.

That view blew my mind. She didn't say no one should ask for a raise. Instead, she understood that the company wasn't obligated to fulfill new needs. My co-worker initially wasted valuable time hurt and angry about the company's decision, but finally recognized that no one else was responsible for the things she wanted in life and moved on to something that better suited her.

The sooner you realize it's irrelevant whether your company's behavior is fair or not, the sooner you can take complete ownership of your life.

Getting angry about what people should or shouldn't do for us or others holds us back while they are moving on. We could be taking action to fulfill our own wants and needs instead of wasting time frustrated with those who aren't doing it for us. By making yourself accountable, you reclaim power back over your life.

What an awful thing we do to others. We put our happiness, finances, and future in their hands – many of these people we wouldn't trust with our goldfish. While many find pleasure in supporting you as you create your best life, no one asked to be responsible for the outcome. We can teach others how to treat us by how we mirror our energy and confidence, but we cannot expect them to carry us because we gave up our ability to carry ourselves.

END THE SENTENCE

No matter what external factors impact your career, you are the common denominator in all of them. The highs and lows of the economy, the family members you took time off to care for, your partner leaving, and your company downsizing are all just constant meteors that are bouncing in and out of your orbit trying to knock you off track. During the journey, you control where you land based on your decisions, actions, and reactions.

If you think retiring within the next few years will be too difficult because of the economy or because you have to take care of your parents, then you are right. Not because of the economy or your parents, but because you've already given yourself the excuses you need to justify falling short. It may be more difficult, but regardless of your obstacles, someone overcame them. Someone did it tired. Someone did it because they couldn't afford not to. Someone did it, even though it wasn't fair they had to. Someone found a smarter way to do it instead of saying it can't be done. With commitment and a made-up mind, it's possible to achieve the difficult.

Fear of a recession hits on a regular cycle. I have chosen to opt out. I don't take part in recessions. I can't afford to. The news tells me the stock market is crashing, property values are dropping, many are losing their job, etc. All of that is awful, and I look for ways I can help, but then I turn the news off. I prefer to spend my time finding new opportunities rather than spend my time in fear of losing my job or worry about tenants not paying. There's nothing I can do until something happens so I choose to keep moving forward building a bigger safety net to prepare for those meteors that hit out of the blue.

The first refinance boom I worked through fell in the middle of the great recession. While flying for work, I met a man who owned a postcard marketing company. After sharing what I did, he told me loan officers were one of his target clients. He asked how business was, and I told him I had a hard time keeping up with incoming business. He replied that half the loan officers he meets say the same, and the other half complain about their struggles to make ends meet due to the recession. We were all working during the same economic collapse, but half had bought into the doom and gloom while the rest found the opportunities.

Blaming the economy allows people to justify their reduction in effort. They've given the economy some of their power by accepting the excuses. While economic factors can certainly play a role in the results, many find success in any market. Many don't. Those who don't may choose to blame the company they work for, yet that same company will likely have one or more top producers. One salesman goes all in regardless of the external factors, while the other embraces every excuse. The company is the same.

So, if you get laid off, if your company shuts down, or you get hit with any other meteor, it's time to end the sentence.

I got laid off. Done.

I closed my company. Next.

I made a mistake. It's over.

You could say, "Like everyone else, I was laid off due to the economy." 'Like everyone else' may make you feel better, but that phrase also releases you from some of the responsibility to better prepare you for the next meteor. You'll look for your next job, but will you take full responsibility for your life and also start that side business you've been thinking about or buy a rental property to prepare for the future? There will be another recession, possibly another lay off, definitely another meteor.

You were laid off. Your partner hurt you. Your family members lied to you. End of sentence. Leave out any justifications that may protect your ego, but prevent you from taking full ownership of tackling what's next. Let the truth anger you and fire you up into long-term action.

Own your life. It's yours. Knowing and understanding that is liberating, not just to you, but to all the others you have been giving your power too. No matter your past, your knowledge, or your experience, there is no one better suited to have complete control and responsibility for your life than you.

13

PEACE AND BALANCE

The days will pass. Soon it will be one year from now, and before you know it, it will be five years from now, ten years, and so on. Will you be where you want to be in that time? Have you even defined where that is so you know when you get there? You don't need to make large, monumental, overwhelming changes. Start with $1 if your goal is to save $1,000. Start with the smallest credit card if your goal is to pay off your debt. Start with one book before bedtime if your goal is to be more present with your children.

The same is true of the disciplines. Start with one thing you can do each morning to add a little calm, focus, and clarity to your life. Then add the next. Trust yourself to know the right discipline needed. If you need to calm your mind, try meditation. If feeling angry or anxious all the time, pick up journaling and start unloading your thoughts.

These disciplines will make you the best version of yourself, but if you want to reach balance, it's important to practice disciplines with specific intentions in each of the 4 Areas of Life. By clearly defining your direction in life and setting consistent goals for the spiritual and emotional, physical, personal connections, and financial, not only will you achieve your personal goals, you will also bring your mind and body into a state of peace and balance. Even if you are far from achieving the end result, you will find peace and balance in the journey.

What small, uncomfortable task can you start today that will put you in a better position a year from now? Those hustling, sacrificing, and bettering themselves today will be closer to a comfortable future. While those spending impulsively, working the minimum, and allowing fear to dictate their decisions will find themselves uncomfortable later in life. Those who created multiple income streams will be alright when their main source of income incurs a hiccup or they desire a career change after reflection. It's never too late to plunge into new discomfort so you can find yourself comfortable years from now.

DECIDE AND MOVE ON

As you begin these disciplines and learn to bet on yourself, it's important to decide who you are becoming. Hustling is not the same as being a workaholic. Hustlers use the energy and opportunity they have right now as it may not be there later. And they don't wait for the energy and opportunity either – they create it. After twenty-plus years of hustle, discomfort, and making the next phone call when I didn't want to, I now get to choose how much energy and opportunity I want to expend. I chase and create only what excites me. A large portion of mortgage professionals have been laid off. Many others have seen a significant decrease in income. Worry and fear dominate the industry. I'd been there and chose not to go back, so I created something years ago that is paying off now and allowing me to move into my reflective phase.

Your 'years ago' will be in a few years. What will you create today to prepare yourself for later?

Don't view your decision as good or bad. Some decisions are simply common sense, others require you follow your moral compass, but the rest of the decisions are just decisions. Each will have results and consequences, and you can only do your best to minimize the latter. If the decision doesn't work out, move on to the next one to be made. The goal is to make decisions that result in the most amount of fulfillment with the least amount of pain long-term.

Avoiding consequences, taking short cuts, sacrificing integrity, or not weighing the risks are the best ways to make a decision worse. Once, a client threatened my reputation online because he couldn't get the loan approval he had expected. To be fair, it was our fault. Some paperwork had gotten misplaced and jeopardized his loan and he was irate. The damage was done and I had two choices: I could craft a few good excuses to limit the aftermath, or I could tell him the truth.

I settled on acknowledging that we dropped the ball and accepted blame. Silence filled the phone before a calm "thank you" came from the other end of the line. The client didn't want lies and excuses, he wanted to be treated with respect. We all do. We discussed our game plan to move forward and I was stunned to receive a five-star review after closing. Avoiding the truth would have been comfortable short-term, but could have resulted in a negative outcome to future business.

Once the choice has been made, own it and move on, regardless of the result. You can't always predict your decision will lead to a better outcome, but there is no need to justify it to others or regret it years from now. Overthinking will paralyze you and drain you of valuable energy.

You must protect your energy at all costs! Your energy is what helps you accomplish great things. It enables you to become a great parent, friend, and co-worker, and allows you to achieve all the things you want in life. If you dedicate too much energy to decision making, you won't have enough left for the things that matter.

HINDSIGHT IS IRRELEVANT

A couple of years ago, my mom said something that blind-sided me while on the phone chatting about the kids and life. She seemed pleased that everyone was happy and healthy even though I chose a different path than she did. She had been a stay-at-home mom throughout my childhood. She woke my brother and I every morning for school, cleaned the house while we were gone, prepared a home-cooked dinner from scratch, and put us to bed at night. There wasn't a day she wasn't there from beginning to end. Assuming she was exactly where she wanted to be, I never viewed it as a sacrifice.

She said, "You know, I wish I would have worked outside the home. I thought I was being a good mom by always being there for you and your brother, but I don't think it made a difference to be around that much. I would've liked a job."

After the initial shock, hearing her words put all of my decisions in a different perspective. No matter what we choose, we may not see the full extent of the rewards or consequences for years to come. We may choose a parenting style with the intention of molding our children into certain behaviors as adults, only to see the opposite take effect. Whatever we decide, even with the best of intentions, we won't know the true impact until years later.

If my mom had worked, would she have regretted it and wished she stayed home?

Maybe.

~~I CAN'T~~ HOW CAN I?

Your life is yours. It should resemble what you envision for yourself. The best way to know what that looks like is to spend time listening to yourself. Be clear about what is important to you – not your parents or your friends, but you. Fear and excuses will constantly try to derail you, but it's up to you to identify, tackle, and overcome each hurdle.

Stop saying, "I can't" when the pressure comes, and start asking, "How can I?" Too many people shut themselves down and fulfill the 'I can't do it' prophecy just by saying those words. Simply asking the question 'how' opens the door to finding creative ways to solve the problem instead. 'I can't' comes from a place of scarcity and puts a limit on what you can achieve. 'How can I' shifts that mindset to abundance and allows you to find ways to do all the things you want to do.

When you can find a way to calm the 'I can't' panic, many times you will see that you are already doing it! You have a lot on your plate, yet you already manage it daily. You are a rockstar, but instead of taking the time to recognize it, you worry about making a mistake, and other kinds of problems that likely never happen, or won't matter if they do.

Celebrate your victories – no matter how small. Use mistakes to learn. Prepare yourself mentally to continue doing the amazing things you are already doing instead of quitting and staying comfortable. You now have the tools, it's up to you to execute.

MAKE DECISIONS – NOT REACTIONS

The practices and disciplines I've shared do more than build wealth and manage stress, they transform numerous areas of your life – including your mind. This transformation of your mind will protect your mental health, which should always be our number one priority. If your mental health isn't in a good place, then wealth, relationships, and energy won't matter.

Protecting your mental health isn't just about removing the toxic. It's about learning to regulate your response to that toxic. You may not be able to remove an offensive family member, or quit a job that sucks the life from your soul. And since you can't shelter yourself from conflict at all times, conquering your reactions is a must.

While many mental health struggles require medical attention (which should be sought immediately if needed), the right mindset is a good way to supplement the medical support.

Developing your mindset gives you the ability to turn reactions into decisions and start building mental toughness. You can begin by implementing the 'how can I' technique, and pretty soon you'll be able to do things like:

Be alone with yourself – The ability to be alone with yourself is the ultimate sign of self-acceptance. Worry, doubt, and intrusive thoughts tend to consume you in the quiet hours, but with practice, and asking yourself 'how can I,' being alone will get easier.

Support those who get what you want – Whether it's the promotion, the 'perfect partner', or the pregnancy, it can be difficult to hide your disappointment when it's not you. It won't be easy, but starting with 'how can I' questions open the door to finding ways to be supportive even while navigating your own pain.

Eliminate comparison to others – Comparison is the easiest way to dismantle your growth. It places attention on what you think you lack or how you fall short, instead of how fortunate you are and how far you've come. You smother your strengths by longing to improve your weaknesses. It's time to ask, 'how can I stop chasing others' performances?'

Seek help – We've all had feelings we couldn't make sense of and we become stuck. The stuck spirals into something we can't see objectively to find a way out of. Whether it's a friend to talk to, or a professional who can guide us through these times, there is nothing too big or small to seek help for – long before losing hope.

The ability to seek guidance when needed, yet trust yourself as the final decision-maker will take your life to a whole new level. There's peace knowing when decisions are made from your best self, and grace when you screw things up.

Your best self always forms a decision – not a reaction.

HOW TO HUSTLE

"Never put off for tomorrow what you can cancel." Wise words from Darren Hardy.

It's simple. Don't keep things on your list that don't need to be done, or at least done by you. Look at your list. Is it really a to-do list, or did you just go down a rabbit hole adding things that make you feel important or productive? Maybe you were just trying to fulfil the 'I can't do it all' prophecy. Start crossing off the tasks you can cancel.

The opposite is also true. Make time for the things that bring you joy, whether profitable or not.

In my twenties, I loved going to flea markets, garage sales, and anywhere I could find items to sell for a profit online. The profits were small, many times under ten dollars a sale, but the adrenaline rush watching a bidding war couldn't be replicated. I loved the thrill of the hunt for new items, getting to know the owners of these items, and hearing other buyers share their knickknack flipping stories.

This pastime made me happy. I wasn't expecting financial success from it, but that was what helped make this hobby so fulfilling – there were no expectations. Around this same time, I was also looking to grow my career, so I asked a co-worker how I could mimic his success in the mortgage industry. I was ready to learn and follow any advice given.

After he shared some excellent tips, he asked what I did in my spare time. Excited, I told him about my cool hobby and the people I got to meet. He recommended I stop "wasting my time with garbage at garage sales, and start thinking about things that matter.

Successful people don't pick up pennies on their way to collect dollars." He proceeded to explain that the money I make at my real job will bring more fulfillment than searching for "junk," and I could use that time calling more clients.

Sadly, that was the day I quit going to flea markets. I believed I had to sacrifice all of my hobbies in order to become a successful loan officer, which I thought would make me a success in life.

I got lost in the hustle. I knew I had to hustle early on, but didn't know how to. So when I envisioned the life I wanted, I sought advice from others, only to realize years later their way was not my way.

Hustling was never the problem, how I hustled was. I hope this book not only teaches you the importance of hustle, but how to hustle.

Embrace hustle and the obstacles that come with it. Hustle in the things that bring you joy. Hustle in the things that keep you healthy, keep you connected to those you love, to yourself, and to everything around you.

I want nothing more for you than to live a life you'd want your children to live. A life that inspires others how to live, and a life full of passion. Live clearly, and live intentionally so you can go all in – without losing yourself.

www.ingramcontent.com/pod-product-compliance
Lightning Source LLC
LaVergne TN
LVHW052025080426
835513LV00018B/2161